CICERO

Pro Archia Poeta Oratio

2nd edition

Teacher's Guide

by

Linda A. Fabrizio

Bolchazy-Carducci Publishers, Inc.
Wauconda, Illinois USA

General Editor:
LeaAnn A. Osburn

Cover Design
Adam Phillip Velez

Cover illustration:
This denarius, minted in Rome ca. 66 BCE by Q. Pomponius Musa,
is one of a series of nine types, each depicting on its reverse
one of the nine muses. Shown here is Calliope, the Muse of epic
poetry, playing the lyre while resting it on a column.
(Photograph courtesy of the American Numismatic Society)

Cicero
Pro Archia Poeta Oratio, 2nd editon
Teacher's Guide

Linda A. Fabrizio

Bolchazy-Carducci Publishers, Inc.
1000 Brown Street
Wauconda, IL 60084 USA
www.bolchazy.com

Printed in the United States of America
2006
by United Graphics

ISBN-13: 978-0-86516-616-5
ISBN-10: 0-86516-616-1

CONTENTS

PREFACE

In this guide, teachers will find the Latin text of the oration in large print suitable for photo-copying, a translation of the oration, a set of assessments with sample answers, and a selected bibliography.

The assessments feature three distinct types of questions: short answer questions, other questions, and essay questions. The short answer questions are often written in the format of the "spot" questions on the AP* Examinations, but certain questions that are basic to general comprehension of the oration are also included. The questions called "other questions" focus mainly on grammar questions about forms and uses, sometimes with a few items for the student to translate. Although these types of questions are not specifically included on the Advanced Placement Examination, it seemed appropriate to include them in this manual to

(a) aid the student with overall translation skills;

(b) remind the student of forms and syntax as the link to an accurate translation;

(c) help improve performance on the multiple choice section of the Advanced Placement Exam.

Essay questions are included periodically in the assessments in order to give the students practice with writing the type of essay included on the Advanced Placement Examinations. When students are asked to consider more than one section of the oration in an essay question, the earlier section is reproduced for the student's ease of reference.

In both the short answer questions and the essay questions, teachers should consistently remind students to cite the Latin that will support their statements. This citation should be bracketed, either by giving line numbers or by giving the first and last word of the Latin, and the Latin should be translated or paraphrased.

After the sample assessments that may be photocopied for use in the classroom, the next section of this teacher guide features the assessment questions followed by answers in bold type. These answers, especially for the essay questions and many of the short answer questions, do not attempt to include every possible answer but are instead offered as a starting point for the teacher's own consideration of what type of answer will be considered acceptable.

Cicero's Latin is a challenge even for the student who has studied the language for three years or more. It is important for the teacher to make good use of the notes in the student text and to break down the long periodic sentences into workable units. This kind of analysis, when done slowly at the outset, can be incorporated more efficiently as the year moves along.

It is also helpful to remind the students that these words were meant to be spoken and the audience had the additional benefit of watching Cicero "in action," with all his gestures and movements, and of hearing the rise and fall of his voice. Experiencing the oration on the written page is much the same as reading rather than seeing Shakespeare.

---

* AP is a registered trademark of the College Entrance Examination Board, which was not involved in the production of, and does not endorse, this product.

It is not easy for students, as they come into the Latin classroom from their various modern subjects, to make the transition to the world of no computers, television, recorded music, instant communication via the internet, cellphones, etc. Thus it is important for the teacher to recreate the scene of Rome during the late Republic as accurately and as vividly as possible. Such an approach will make Cicero's words come alive. Students can take virtual tours of ancient Rome and the Forum Romanum online rather easily. Sometimes simply having one image displayed for the class can help create the scene immediately. Teachers can also draw the obvious analogies to current courtroom cases, politicians, and public figures.

The *pro Archia* does provide the teacher with good opportunities to discuss the values of a society, and, in particular, how Cicero tried to stress what he considered to be most important in life—the role of the artist, and how society treats its artists. These are topics on which all students can comment.

Finally, a note of thanks to Professor William Mayer of Hunter College, and colleagues Patsy Ricks and Krista Irwin for their helpful comments on the translation and assessments. Your generosity is most appreciated.

Linda A. Fabrizio
Garden City High School
January, 2006

LARGE SIZE TEXT OF THE ORATION

M. TULLI CICERONIS
PRO ARCHIA
POETA ORATIO

EXORDIUM
(1–41)

1 Si quid est in me ingeni, iudices, quod sentio quam sit exiguum, aut si qua exercitatio dicendi, in qua me non infitior mediocriter esse versatum, aut si huiusce rei ratio aliqua ab optimarum artium studiis ac disciplina

5 profecta, a qua ego nullum confiteor aetatis meae tempus abhorruisse, earum rerum omnium vel in primis hic A. Licinius fructum a me repetere prope suo iure debet. Nam quoad longissime potest mens mea respicere spatium praeteriti temporis et pueritiae memoriam recordari

10 ultimam, inde usque repetens hunc video mihi principem et ad suscipiendam et ad ingrediendam rationem horum studiorum exstitisse. Quod si haec vox huius hortatu praeceptisque conformata non nullis aliquando saluti fuit, a quo id accepimus quo ceteris opitulari et alios servare

15 possemus, huic profecto ipsi, quantum est situm in nobis, et opem et salutem ferre debemus. **2** Ac ne quis a nobis hoc ita dici forte miretur, quod alia quaedam in hoc facultas sit ingeni neque haec dicendi ratio aut disciplina, ne nos quidem huic uni studio penitus umquam dediti fuimus.

20 Etenim omnes artes quae ad humanitatem pertinent habent

quoddam commune vinculum et quasi cognatione quadam inter se continentur. **3** Sed ne cui vestrum mirum esse
videatur, me in quaestione legitima et in iudicio publico,
cum res agatur apud praetorem populi Romani, lectissimum
25   virum, et apud severissimos iudices, tanto conventu hominum ac frequentia, hoc uti genere dicendi, quod non
modo a consuetudine iudiciorum, verum etiam a forensi sermone abhorreat, quaeso a vobis ut in hac causa
mihi detis hanc veniam accommodatam huic reo, vobis,
30   quemadmodum spero, non molestam, ut me pro summo
poeta atque eruditissimo homine dicentem hoc concursu
hominum litteratissimorum, hac vestra humanitate, hoc
denique praetore exercente iudicium, patiamini de studiis
humanitatis ac litterarum paulo loqui liberius, et in eius
35   modi persona quae propter otium ac studium minime
in iudiciis periculisque tractata est uti prope novo quodam et inusitato genere dicendi. **4** Quod si mihi a vobis
tribui concedique sentiam, perficiam profecto ut hunc A.
Licinium non modo non segregandum, cum sit civis, a
40   numero civium verum etiam, si non esset, putetis asciscendum fuisse.

NARRATIO
(42–89)

Nam ut primum ex pueris excessit Archias atque ab
eis artibus quibus aetas puerilis ad humanitatem informari
solet, se ad scribendi studium contulit. Primum Antiochiae
45 —nam ibi natus est loco nobili—celebri quondam urbe et
copiosa atque eruditissimis hominibus liberalissimisque
studiis adfluenti, celeriter antecellere omnibus ingeni gloria
coepit. Post in ceteris Asiae partibus cunctaque Graecia sic
eius adventus celebrabantur ut famam ingeni exspectatio
50 hominis, exspectationem ipsius adventus admiratioque
superaret.

5 Erat Italia tum plena Graecarum artium ac disciplinarum, studiaque haec et in Latio vehementius tum
colebantur quam nunc isdem in oppidis, et hic Romae
55 propter tranquillitatem rei publicae non neglegebantur.
Itaque hunc et Tarentini et Locrenses et Regini et Neapolitani civitate ceterisque praemiis donarunt, et omnes
qui aliquid de ingeniis poterant iudicare cognitione atque
hospitio dignum existimarunt. Hac tanta celebritate
60 famae cum esset iam absentibus notus, Romam venit

Mario consule et Catulo. Nactus est primum consules eos quorum alter res ad scribendum maximas, alter cum res gestas tum etiam studium atque auris adhibere posset. Statim Luculli, cum praetextatus etiam tum Archias esset,

65 eum domum suam receperunt. Dedit etiam hoc non solum lumen ingeni ac litterarum, verum etiam naturae atque virtutis ut domus, quae huius adulescentiae prima favit, eadem esset familiarissima senectuti.

6 Erat temporibus illis iucundus Q. Metello, illi

70 Numidico, et eius Pio filio, audiebatur a M. Aemilio, vivebat cum Q. Catulo et patre et filio, a L. Crasso colebatur. Lucullos vero et Drusum et Octavios et Catonem et totam Hortensiorum domum devinctam consuetudine cum teneret, adficiebatur summo honore, quod eum non

75 solum colebant, qui aliquid percipere atque audire studebant, verum etiam si qui forte simulabant. Interim satis longo intervallo, cum esset cum M. Lucullo in Siciliam profectus et cum ex ea provincia cum eodem Lucullo decederet, venit Heracleam. Quae cum esset

80 civitas aequissimo iure ac foedere, ascribi se in eam civitatem voluit idque, cum ipse per se dignus

putaretur, tum auctoritate et gratia Luculli ab Hera-

cliensibus impetravit. **7** Data est civitas Silvani lege et Car-

bonis: Sɪ ǫᴜɪ ꜰᴏᴇᴅᴇʀᴀᴛɪꜱ ᴄɪᴠɪᴛᴀᴛɪʙᴜꜱ ᴀꜱᴄʀɪᴘᴛɪ ꜰᴜɪꜱꜱᴇɴᴛ, ꜱɪ ᴛᴜᴍ

85   ᴄᴜᴍ ʟᴇx ꜰᴇʀᴇʙᴀᴛᴜʀ ɪɴ Iᴛᴀʟɪᴀ ᴅᴏᴍɪᴄɪʟɪᴜᴍ ʜᴀʙᴜɪꜱꜱᴇɴᴛ ᴇᴛ

ꜱɪ ꜱᴇxᴀɢɪɴᴛᴀ ᴅɪᴇʙᴜꜱ ᴀᴘᴜᴅ ᴘʀᴀᴇᴛᴏʀᴇᴍ ᴇꜱꜱᴇɴᴛ ᴘʀᴏꜰᴇꜱꜱɪ.

Cum hic domicilium Romae multos iam annos haberet,

professus est apud praetorem Q. Metellum, familiar-

issimum suum.

REFUTATIO
(90–143)

90   **8** Si nihil aliud nisi de civitate ac lege dicimus, nihil dico amplius: causa dicta est. Quid enim horum infirmari, Gratti, potest? Heracleaene esse tum ascriptum negabis? Adest vir summa auctoritate et religione et fide, M. Lucullus, qui se non opinari sed scire, non

95   audisse sed vidisse, non interfuisse sed egisse dicit. Adsunt Heraclienses legati, nobilissimi homines, huius iudici causa cum mandatis et cum publico testimonio venerunt, qui hunc ascriptum Heracleae esse dicunt. Hic tu tabulas desideras Heracliensium publicas, quas Italico bello

100 incenso tabulario interisse scimus omnes? Est ridiculum ad ea quae habemus nihil dicere, quaerere quae habere non possumus, et de hominum memoria tacere, litterarum memoriam flagitare et, cum habeas amplissimi viri religionem, integerrimi municipi ius iurandum fidemque,

105 ea quae depravari nullo modo possunt repudiare, tabulas quas idem dicis solere corrumpi desiderare.

    9 An domicilium Romae non habuit is qui tot annis ante civitatem datam sedem omnium rerum ac fortunarum suarum Romae conlocavit? An non est professus? Immo

110   vero eis tabulis professus quae solae ex illa professione
conlegioque praetorum obtinent publicarum tabularum
auctoritatem. Nam, cum Appi tabulae neglegentius adservatae dicerentur, Gabini, quam diu incolumis fuit,
levitas, post damnationem calamitas omnem tabularum

115   fidem resignasset, Metellus, homo sanctissimus modestissimusque omnium, tanta diligentia fuit ut ad L. Lentulum praetorem et ad iudices venerit et unius nominis
litura se commotum esse dixerit. His igitur in tabulis
nullam lituram in nomine A. Licini videtis. **10** Quae cum

120   ita sint, quid est quod de eius civitate dubitetis, praesertim cum aliis quoque in civitatibus fuerit ascriptus? Etenim cum mediocribus multis et aut nulla aut humili aliqua
arte praeditis gratuito civitatem in Graecia homines impertiebant, Reginos credo aut Locrensis aut Neapolitanos

125   aut Tarentinos, quod scaenicis artificibus largiri solebant, id
huic summa ingeni praedito gloria noluisse! Quid? Cum
ceteri non modo post civitatem datam sed etiam post legem Papiam aliquo modo in eorum municipiorum tabulas inrepserunt, hic qui ne utitur quidem illis in quibus

130   est scriptus, quod semper se Heracliensem esse voluit, reicietur? **11** Census nostros requiris. Scilicet! Est

enim obscurum proximis censoribus hunc cum clarissimo imperatore L. Lucullo apud exercitum fuisse, superioribus cum eodem quaestore fuisse in Asia, primis

135 Iulio et Crasso nullam populi partem esse censam.
Sed, quoniam census non ius civitatis confirmat ac tantum
modo indicat eum, qui sit census, ita se iam tum gessisse pro
cive, eis temporibus is quem tu criminaris ne ipsius quidem
iudicio in civium Romanorum iure esse versatum et testa-

140 mentum saepe fecit nostris legibus, et adiit hereditates civium
Romanorum, et in beneficiis ad aerarium delatus est a L. Lucullo pro consule. Quaere argumenta, si quae potes; numquam
enim hic neque suo neque amicorum iudicio revincetur.

CONFIRMATIO
(144–375)

12 Quaeres a nobis, Gratti, cur tanto opere hoc

145   homine delectemur. Quia suppeditat nobis ubi et animus

ex hoc forensi strepitu reficiatur et aures convicio defessae

conquiescant. An tu existimas aut suppetere nobis posse

quod cotidie dicamus in tanta varietate rerum, nisi animos

nostros doctrina excolamus, aut ferre animos tantam posse

150   contentionem, nisi eos doctrina eadem relaxemus? Ego

vero fateor me his studiis esse deditum. Ceteros pudeat,

si qui ita se litteris abdiderunt ut nihil possint ex eis neque

ad communem adferre fructum neque in aspectum lu-

cemque proferre; me autem quid pudeat qui tot annos ita

155   vivo, iudices, ut a nullius umquam me tempore aut com-

modo aut otium meum abstraxerit aut voluptas avocarit

aut denique somnus retardarit? **13** Quare quis tandem me

reprehendat, aut quis mihi iure suscenseat, si, quantum ce-

teris ad suas res obeundas, quantum ad festos dies ludorum

160   celebrandos, quantum ad alias voluptates et ad ipsam re-

quiem animi et corporis conceditur temporum, quantum alii

tribuunt tempestivis conviviis, quantum denique alveolo,

quantum pilae, tantum mihi egomet ad haec studia recolenda

sumpsero? Atque id eo mihi concedendum est magis quod

165 ex his studiis haec quoque crescit oratio et facultas quae, quantacumque est in me, numquam amicorum periculis defuit. Quae si cui levior videtur, illa quidem certe quae summa sunt ex quo fonte hauriam sentio. **14** Nam nisi multorum praeceptis multisque litteris mihi ab adulescentia

170 suasissem nihil esse in vita magno opere expetendum nisi laudem atque honestatem, in ea autem persequenda omnis cruciatus corporis, omnia pericula mortis atque exsili parvi esse ducenda, numquam me pro salute vestra in tot ac tantas dimicationes atque in hos profligatorum hominum

175 cotidianos impetus obiecissem. Sed pleni omnes sunt libri, plenae sapientium voces, plena exemplorum vetustas; quae iacerent in tenebris omnia, nisi litterarum lumen accederet. Quam multas nobis imagines non solum ad intuendum verum etiam ad imitandum fortissimorum virorum

180 expressas scriptores et Graeci et Latini reliquerunt! Quas ego mihi semper in administranda re publica proponens animum et mentem meam ipsa cogitatione hominum excellentium conformabam.

15 Quaeret quispiam: "Quid? Illi ipsi summi viri,

185 quorum virtutes litteris proditae sunt, istane doctrina

quam tu effers laudibus eruditi fuerunt?" Difficile est hoc de omnibus confirmare, sed tamen est certum quid respondeam. Ego multos homines excellenti animo ac virtute fuisse et sine doctrina, naturae ipsius habitu prope

190 divino per se ipsos et moderatos et gravis exstitisse fateor; etiam illud adiungo: saepius ad laudem atque virtutem naturam sine doctrina quam sine natura valuisse doctrinam. Atque idem ego hoc contendo: cum ad naturam eximiam et inlustrem accesserit ratio quaedam conformatioque

195 doctrinae, tum illud nescioquid praeclarum ac singulare solere exsistere. **16** Ex hoc esse hunc numero quem patres nostri viderunt, divinum hominem, Africanum, ex hoc C. Laelium, L. Furium, moderatissimos homines et continentissimos, ex hoc fortissimum virum et illis

200 temporibus doctissimum, M. Catonem illum senem. Qui profecto si nihil ad percipiendam colendamque virtutem litteris adiuvarentur, numquam se ad earum studium contulissent. Quod si non hic tantus fructus ostenderetur, et si ex his studiis delectatio sola peteretur, tamen,

205 ut opinor, hanc animi remissionem humanissimam ac liberalissimam iudicaretis. Nam ceterae neque temporum sunt

neque aetatum omnium neque locorum; at haec studia adulescentiam acuunt, senectutem oblectant, secundas res
ornant, adversis perfugium ac solacium praebent, delectant

210 domi, non impediunt foris, pernoctant nobiscum, peregrinantur, rusticantur.

17 Quod si ipsi haec neque attingere neque sensu nostro gustare possemus, tamen ea mirari deberemus, etiam
cum in aliis videremus. Quis nostrum tam animo agresti ac

215 duro fuit ut Rosci morte nuper non commoveretur? qui
cum esset senex mortuus, tamen propter excellentem artem ac venustatem videbatur omnino mori non debuisse.
Ergo ille corporis motu tantum amorem sibi conciliarat a nobis
omnibus; nos animorum incredibilis motus celeritatemque

220 ingeniorum neglegemus? **18** Quotiens ego hunc Archiam
vidi, iudices—utar enim vestra benignitate, quoniam me
in hoc novo genere dicendi tam diligenter attenditis—quotiens ego hunc vidi, cum litteram scripsisset nullam, magnum numerum optimorum versuum de eis ipsis rebus

225 quae tum agerentur dicere ex tempore, quotiens revocatum eandem rem dicere commutatis verbis atque sententiis! Quae vero accurate cogitateque scripsisset, ea sic vidi

probari ut ad veterum scriptorum laudem perveniret. Hunc ego non diligam, non admirer, non omni ratione

230 defendendum putem? Atque sic a summis hominibus eruditissimisque accepimus, ceterarum rerum studia ex doctrina et praeceptis et arte constare, poetam natura ipsa valere et mentis viribus excitari et quasi divino quodam spiritu inflari. Quare suo iure noster ille Ennius "sanctos"

235 appellat poetas, quod quasi deorum aliquo dono atque munere commendati nobis esse videantur.

19 Sit igitur, iudices, sanctum apud vos, humanissimos homines, hoc poetae nomen quod nulla umquam barbaria violavit. Saxa atque solitudines voci

240 respondent, bestiae saepe immanes cantu flectuntur atque consistunt; nos instituti rebus optimis non poetarum voce moveamur? Homerum Colophonii civem esse dicunt suum, Chii suum vindicant, Salaminii repetunt, Smyrnaei vero suum esse confirmant itaque etiam delubrum eius in

245 oppido dedicaverunt, permulti alii praeterea pugnant inter se atque contendunt. Ergo illi alienum, quia poeta fuit, post mortem etiam expetunt; nos hunc vivum qui et voluntate et legibus noster est repudiamus, praesertim cum omne olim

studium atque omne ingenium contulerit Archias ad populi

250 Romani gloriam laudemque celebrandam? Nam et Cimbricas res adulescens attigit et ipsi illi C. Mario qui durior ad haec studia videbatur iucundus fuit. **20** Neque
enim quisquam est tam aversus a Musis qui non mandari
versibus aeternum suorum laborum praeconium facile

255 patiatur. Themistoclem illum, summum Athenis virum,
dixisse aiunt, cum ex eo quaereretur quod acroama aut
cuius vocem libentissime audiret: eius a quo sua virtus
optime praedicaretur. Itaque ille Marius item eximie L.
Plotium dilexit, cuius ingenio putabat ea quae gesserat

260 posse celebrari. **21** Mithridaticum vero bellum magnum
atque difficile et in multa varietate terra marique versatum
totum ab hoc expressum est; qui libri non modo L. Lucullum, fortissimum et clarissimum virum, verum etiam
populi Romani nomen inlustrant. Populus enim Romanus

265 aperuit Lucullo imperante Pontum et regiis quondam opibus
et ipsa natura et regione vallatum, populi Romani exercitus
eodem duce non maxima manu innumerabilis Armeniorum
copias fudit, populi Romani laus est urbem amicissimam
Cyzicenorum eiusdem consilio ex omni impetu regio atque

270   totius belli ore ac faucibus ereptam esse atque servatam. Nostra semper feretur et praedicabitur L. Lucullo dimicante, cum interfectis ducibus depressa hostium classis est, incredibilis apud Tenedum pugna illa navalis, nostra sunt tropaea, nostra monumenta, nostri triumphi. Quae

275   quorum ingeniis efferuntur, ab eis populi Romani fama celebratur.

22 Carus fuit Africano superiori noster Ennius, itaque etiam in sepulcro Scipionum putatur is esse constitutus ex marmore. At eis laudibus certe non solum

280   ipse qui laudatur sed etiam populi Romani nomen ornatur. In caelum huius proavus Cato tollitur; magnus honos populi Romani rebus adiungitur. Omnes denique illi Maximi, Marcelli, Fulvii non sine communi omnium nostrum laude decorantur. Ergo illum qui haec fecerat,

285   Rudinum hominem, maiores nostri in civitatem receperunt; nos hunc Heracliensem, multis civitatibus expetitum, in hac autem legibus constitutum, de nostra civitate eiciamus?

23 Nam si quis minorem gloriae fructum putat ex Graecis versibus percipi quam ex Latinis, vehementer errat,

290   propterea quod Graeca leguntur in omnibus fere gentibus,

Latina suis finibus exiguis sane continentur. Quare, si res eae quas gessimus orbis terrae regionibus definiuntur, cupere debemus, quo hominum nostrorum tela pervenerint, eodem gloriam famamque penetrare, quod cum ipsis

295 populis de quorum rebus scribitur haec ampla sunt, tum eis certe qui de vita gloriae causa dimicant hoc maximum et periculorum incitamentum est et laborum. **24** Quam multos scriptores rerum suarum magnus ille Alexander secum habuisse dicitur. Atque is tamen, cum in Sigeo

300 ad Achillis tumulum astitisset: "O fortunate," inquit, "adulescens, qui tuae virtutis Homerum praeconem inveneris!" Et vere: nam nisi Ilias illa exstitisset, idem tumulus qui corpus eius contexerat nomen etiam obruisset. Quid? Noster hic Magnus qui cum virtute fortunam

305 adaequavit, nonne Theophanem Mytilenaeum, scriptorem rerum suarum, in contione militum civitate donavit, et nostri illi fortes viri, sed rustici ac milites, dulcedine quadam gloriae commoti quasi participes eiusdem laudis magno illud clamore approbaverunt?

310   **25** Itaque, credo, si civis Romanus Archias legibus non esset, ut ab aliquo imperatore civitate donaretur perficere non potuit. Sulla cum Hispanos et Gallos donaret,

credo, hunc petentem repudiasset. Quem nos in contione vidimus, cum ei libellum malus poeta de populo
315   subiecisset, quod epigramma in eum fecisset tantum modo
alternis versibus longiusculis, statim ex eis rebus, quas tum
vendebat, iubere ei praemium tribui—sed ea condicione
ne quid postea scriberet. Qui sedulitatem mali poetae
duxerit aliquo tamen praemio dignam, huius ingenium et
320   virtutem in scribendo et copiam non expetisset? **26** Quid? a
Q. Metello Pio, familiarissimo suo, qui civitate multos donavit, neque per se neque per Lucullos impetravisset? qui
praesertim usque eo de suis rebus scribi cuperet ut etiam
Cordubae natis poetis pingue quiddam sonantibus atque
325   peregrinum tamen auris suas dederet. Neque enim est hoc
dissimulandum quod obscurari non potest, sed prae nobis ferendum: trahimur omnes studio laudis, et optimus
quisque maxime gloria ducitur. Ipsi illi philosophi etiam
in eis libellis quos de contemnenda gloria scribunt nomen
330   suum inscribunt; in eo ipso in quo praedicationem nobilitatemque despiciunt praedicari de se ac nominari
volunt. **27** Decimus quidem Brutus, summus vir et imperator, Acci, amicissimi sui, carminibus templorum ac
monumentorum aditus exornavit suorum. Iam vero ille qui

335   cum Aetolis Ennio comite bellavit Fulvius non dubitavit
       Martis manubias Musis consecrare. Quare, in qua urbe
       imperatores prope armati poetarum nomen et Mu-
       sarum delubra coluerunt, in ea non debent togati iudi-
       ces a Musarum honore et a poetarum salute abhorrere.

340   **28** Atque ut id libentius faciatis, iam me vobis, iudi-
       ces, indicabo et de meo quodam amore gloriae nimis acri
       fortasse, verum tamen honesto vobis confitebor. Nam quas
       res nos in consulatu nostro vobiscum simul pro salute hui-
       us urbis atque imperi et pro vita civium proque universa

345   re publica gessimus, attigit hic versibus atque inchoavit.
       Quibus auditis, quod mihi magna res et iucunda visa est,
       hunc ad perficiendum adornavi. Nullam enim virtus aliam
       mercedem laborum periculorumque desiderat praeter hanc
       laudis et gloriae. Qua quidem detracta, iudices, quid est

350   quod in hoc tam exiguo vitae curriculo et tam brevi tan-
       tis nos in laboribus exerceamus? **29** Certe, si nihil animus
       praesentiret in posterum, et si, quibus regionibus vitae
       spatium circumscriptum est, isdem omnis cogitationes ter-
       minaret suas, nec tantis se laboribus frangeret neque tot

355   curis vigiliisque angeretur nec totiens de ipsa vita
       dimicaret. Nunc insidet quaedam in optimo quoque virtus,

quae noctes ac dies animum gloriae stimulis concitat atque admonet non cum vitae tempore esse dimitten-dam commemorationem nominis nostri, sed cum omni

360 posteritate adaequandam. **30** An vero tam parvi animi videamur esse omnes qui in re publica atque in his vi-tae periculis laboribusque versamur ut, cum usque ad extremum spatium nullum tranquillum atque otiosum spiritum duxerimus, nobiscum simul moritura omnia

365 arbitremur? An statuas et imagines, non animorum simulacra, sed corporum, studiose multi summi homines reliquerunt; consiliorum relinquere ac virtutum nostrarum effigiem nonne multo malle debemus summis ingeniis ex-pressam et politam? Ego vero omnia quae gerebam iam

370 tum in gerendo spargere me ac disseminare arbitrabar in orbis terrae memoriam sempiternam. Haec vero sive a meo sensu post mortem afutura est, sive, ut sapientis-simi homines putaverunt, ad aliquam animi mei partem pertinebit, nunc quidem certe cogitatione quadam speque delector.

PERORATIO
(376–397)

31 Quare conservate, iudices, hominem pudore eo quem amicorum videtis comprobari cum dignitate, tum etiam vetustate, ingenio autem tanto quantum id convenit existimari, quod summorum hominum iudiciis expetitum 380 esse videatis, causa vero eius modi quae beneficio legis, auctoritate municipi, testimonio Luculli, tabulis Metelli comprobetur. Quae cum ita sint, petimus a vobis, iudices, si qua non modo humana verum etiam divina in tantis ingeniis commendatio debet esse, ut eum qui vos, qui 385 vestros imperatores, qui populi Romani res gestas semper ornavit, qui etiam his recentibus nostris vestrisque domesticis periculis aeternum se testimonium laudis daturum esse profitetur, quique est ex eo numero qui semper apud omnis sancti sunt habiti itaque dicti, sic in 390 vestram accipiatis fidem ut humanitate vestra levatus potius quam acerbitate violatus esse videatur.

32 Quae de causa pro mea consuetudine breviter simpliciterque dixi, iudices, ea confido probata esse omnibus; quae a foro aliena iudicialique consuetudine et

395   de hominis ingenio et communiter de ipso studio locutus sum, ea, iudices, a vobis spero esse in bonam partem accepta, ab eo qui iudicium exercet, certo scio.

TRANSLATION OF THE ORATION

EXORDIUM
(1–41)

1 If there is anything of talent in me, jury, which I realize how slight it is, or if there is any practice of speaking, in which I do not deny that I have been moderately engaged, or if there is some strategy of this case before us derived from the pursuits and training of the best liberal arts, to which I confess that no time of my life has been adverse, here Aulus Licinius especially ought, by a right nearly his own, to seek in return from me a benefit of all these things. For as far as possible as my mind is able to look back at an interval of a previous time and is able to recall a memory of childhood, searching from that point on, I see that for me this man stood out as foremost for the purpose of undertaking and of embarking on a course of these studies. But if this voice (of mine), trained by the encouragement and teaching of this man, has been a source of safety for any, surely I ought, as much as is in my power, to bring both aid and safety to this very man from whom I have received that by which I can give help to some and to save others. **2** And lest anyone by chance wonder that this is being spoken in this way by me, because there is another certain skill of a natural talent in this man and not this system of or training in speaking, (let me mention that) not even I have ever been thoroughly devoted to this one pursuit. Indeed, all the liberal studies which relate to civilization have a certain common bond and are held together among themselves by, as it were, a certain kinship. **3** But lest it seem to be strange to any of you that, in a legal investigation and in a public trial, (since the matter is being handled in the presence of the praetor of the Roman people, a very well chosen man and before most serious jurors), in so great an assembly and crowd of men, I use this type of speaking which not only is averse to the practice of legal proceedings but also to a style of speaking connected with the Forum, I seek from all of you that in this trial you grant me this indulgence, appropriate for this defendant and, as I hope it is not bothersome for you, that you allow me, speaking on behalf of a very esteemed poet and most educated man in this assembly of very learned men, because of your culture, finally with this praetor presiding, to speak a little more freely about the pursuits of culture and literature, and, in a person of this kind who, on account of a leisure devoted to the liberal arts and study, is least experienced in trials and legal hazards, (you permit me) to use a certain almost new and unusual kind of speaking. **4** But if I should feel that it is bestowed and is granted to me by you, I would bring it about without question that you think that Aulus Licinius here not only should not have been excluded from the number of citizens, since he is a citizen, but also that, if he were not a citizen, you would think that he ought to have been enrolled.

NARRATIO
(42–89)

For as soon as he departed from his boyhood years and from those arts with which the period of boyhood is usually molded for formal society, Archias applied himself to the pursuit of writing. First in Antioch—for there he was born in a noble place—once a populous city and rich, and abounding with very educated men and the most liberal studies—he began quickly to surpass everyone with respect to the fame of his talent. Later in other parts of Asia and in all of Greece, his arrivals were attended in such large numbers that the expectation of the man went beyond the fame of his talent and the admiration (once he arrived) surpassed the expectation of his arrival.

5 Italy was then full of Greek arts and studies and these were fostered in Latium more energetically than now in those same towns, and here in Rome, on account of the calmness of the republic, they were not overlooked. Therefore, both the people of Tarentum and of Locri and of Rhegium and of Naples endowed this man with citizenship and other rewards, and everyone who was able to judge something about his talents thought that he was worthy of recognition and the rights of hospitality. Since he was already known to those absent (far away) because of this so great a renown of his reputation, he came to Rome in the consulship of Marius and Catulus. At first he became attached to the consuls of whom the one was able to provide outstanding achievements for writing about and the other to furnish not only deeds but the enthusiasm and the ears (attention). Immediately, the Luculli received him into their home, although Archias was even then still wearing the *toga praetexta*. Even this gave off not only the light of his talent and literature, but also of his nature and his character, as the house, which first showed favor to him in his youth, was the same very familiar (house) to him in his old age.

6 In those times he was on friendly terms with that famous Quintus Metellus Numidicus, and his son, Pius; he was heard by Marcus Aemilius, he lived with Quintus Catulus, both the father and the son, (and) he was cultivated by Lucius Crassus. Indeed, since he held the Luculli and Drusus and the Octavii and Cato and the entire household of the Hortensii bound by the custom of social ties, he was treated with the highest honor, because they who were eager to hear and learn something (good) not only cherished him, but also if anyone by chance was pretending (to be hearing or learning). In the meantime, after a rather long interval, when he had departed with Marcus Lucullus for Sicily and when he left from that province with that same Lucullus, he came to Heraclea. Since this was a state with a most just law and treaty, he wanted himself to be enrolled into that citizenship and he obtained this from the Heracleans then by the influence and the esteem of Lucullus, although he himself was considered worthy by his own right. **7** Citizenship was granted according to the law of Carbo and Silvanus: IF ANY HAD BEEN ENROLLED IN FEDERATED STATES, IF THEN THEY HAD A RESIDENCE IN ITALY WHEN THE LAW WAS CARRIED OUT AND IF THEY HAD REGISTERED IN FRONT OF A PRAETOR WITHIN SIXTY DAYS. Since he already had a residence here at Rome for many years, he enrolled in front of his very close associate, the praetor Quintus Metellus.

REFUTATIO
(90–143)

8 If I say nothing else except about citizenship and the law, I have nothing more to say: the case has been spoken. For what, Grattius, of these things, can be nullified? Will you say that he was not enrolled at that time in Heraclea? The man, of highest prestige and reverence and loyalty, is here, Marcus Lucullus, who says that he does not think but knows, that he did not hear but he saw, that he was not present but did (these things). There are present Heraclean envoys, noblest men, who on account of this trial have come with mandates and with public testimony, who say that this man was enrolled in Heraclea. Here, do you want the public records of the Heracleans, which we all know have been missing because of the archives building being burned in the Italian war? It is absurd to say nothing (in response) to these things which we do have and to seek those things which we are not able to have, and to be silent about the memory of men (what men remember) to demand the memory of letters (written records) and, when you have the authenticity of a very distinguished man, the oath and fidelity of a very esteemed community, to regard as false those things which in no way can be tampered with, and to desire records which you yourself say are usually falsified.

9 Or did he not have a residence at Rome, he, who so many years before citizenship had been granted, set up a home of all his possessions and wealth at Rome? Whether he did not submit his name? On the contrary, indeed, he enrolled in those records which alone, from that formal declaration and from the board of praetors, possess the authority of public records. For although the records of Appius were said to have been kept somewhat carelessly, [although] the frivolity of Gabinius, who was so long safe from prosecution, [and] the misfortune after his condemnation in a court of law broke the binding force of all faith in the records, Metellus, the most scrupulous and most restrained man of all, was of such great attentiveness that he came to the praetor L. Lentulus and to the jury and said that he was disturbed by the erasure of one name. Therefore in these records you see not any erasure in the name of Aulus Licinius. **10** Since these things are so, what is there which you doubt about his citizenship? Especially since he was enrolled also in other states? Indeed when men in Magna Graecia offered citizenship for nothing to many ordinary men and those endowed with either no or some insignificant skill, I suppose that the people of Rhegium or of Locri or the Neapolitans or the Tarentini did not want to grant this man endowed with a supreme glory of talent that which they were accustomed to conferring upon stage artists! Well? What about when the rest not only in some way slipped in after citizenship had been given but also after the Papian law, will this man be refused who does not even use those (records) in which he was enrolled because he always wanted to be a Heraclean (citizen)? **11** You ask for our census records. To be sure! For it is unclear at the time of the last censors that this man was with the army with the very famous general L. Lucullus, at the time of the previous censors he was in Asia with the same Lucullus as quaestor, and, under the first censors Iulius and Crassus, that not any part of the people were registered in the census. But, since the census does not prove the right of citizenship and only shows that he who has been enrolled at that time conducted himself in such a way as a citizen would, he whom you accuse not even in his own judgment was engaged in the right of Roman citizens, often made a will according to our laws, entered into inheritances of Roman citizens, and was conferred to the treasury in the rewards by the proconsul L. Lucullus. Seek proof, if you are able to find any; for never will this man be convicted of a falsehood neither by his own judgment nor that of his friends.

CONFIRMATIO
(144–375)

12 You will ask from me, Grattius, why I am so greatly charmed by this man. Because he furnishes us (with a place) where both the mind may be refreshed from this noise of the court and the ears, weary from the clamor, might rest. Or do you think that that which we say everyday on such a variety of things can be available to us if we do not cultivate our minds with formal teaching? Or can our minds bear such great conflict unless we relax them with that same teaching? Truly I confess that I have been dedicated to these pursuits. Let it shame the rest, if anyone has hidden themselves in literature in such a way that they derive no benefit from it to bring neither to the common good nor into the view of light. Moreover, why should it shame me however who has lived so many years in such a way, jurors, that my leisure time has not dragged me away nor has entertainment called me away nor finally has sleep inhibited me ever from the time of need or the interest of anyone. **13** Wherefore who finally would blame me, or who would rightly be angry with me, if it is granted how much time is devoted by others for the purpose of carrying out their own affairs, how much time for attending in large crowds the festival days for games, how much time for other pleasures and for rest itself of mind and body, how much others devote to timely dinner parties, finally, how much to the gaming board, how much to playing ball, just as much time I take up for myself for the purpose of resuming these studies? And this ought to be granted to me by so much more that this speech also grows from these studies and the capacity for public speaking which, however much is in me, never has been lacking in the perilous times of my friends. If this seems rather slight to anyone, indeed I perceive from which source I derive those things which are the highest. **14** For if I had not persuaded myself from youth by the instructions of many (teachers) and much literature that nothing was in life to be sought with great effort except praise and integrity, and moreover that every pain of the body in pursuing them, every danger of death and of exile must be considered insignificant, never would I have thrown myself for your safety into so many and such great struggles and into these daily assaults of desperate men. But all the books are full, all the voices of wise men are full, all of tradition is full of examples; which all would lie in darkness if the light of literature did not approach them. How many portraits produced of very brave men both Greek and Latin writers have left for us not only for the purpose of examining but also for imitating. Holding these up to myself always (as models) in administering the state, I used to shape my mind by means of this very reflection of outstanding men.

15 Someone will ask "What? Those very most excellent men whose virtues have been handed down in literature, was it by this kind of education which you lift up with praises that they were instructed?" It is difficult to confirm this about everyone, but nevertheless it is certain what I should answer. I confess that there have been many men of excellent mind and virtue without instruction, by the nearly divine quality of their very natural abilities through themselves they themselves have stood out as restrained and serious; I also add that: more often has natural ability without education had the power to produce praise and virtue rather than education without natural ability. And this same thing I assert: when a certain system of training and education has been added to a special natural ability, at that time that certain something or other is accustomed to emerge. **16** I assert that out of this number is this divine man whom our fathers saw, Africanus, a man of godlike qualities, from this number, Gaius Laelius, Lucius Furius, very restrained and temperate men, from this number, a very brave man and very learned for those times, that Marcus Cato the Elder. Surely if these had been aided in no way by literature for the purpose of acquiring and cultivating virtue, they never would have brought themselves to the pursuit of these things. But if this so great an advantage were not shown, and if from these studies the gaining of pleasure alone was sought, nevertheless, as I think, you would judge this relaxation of the mind as very civilized and very characteristic of a liberal education. For other (kinds of relaxation) are not for all times or places; but these studies sharpen youth, delight old age, adorn favorable circumstances, offer refuge and comfort in adverse times, are a delight at home, do not hinder away from home, spend the night with us, travel, spend time in the country.

17 But if we ourselves should be able neither to touch these things nor taste them with any of our five senses, nevertheless we ought to be amazed at them even when we might see them in others. Who of us was of so coarse and hard a spirit that he was not moved recently by the death of Roscius? Although he died as an old man, nevertheless on account of his outstanding skill and charm, it seemed that he should not in any way have died. Therefore, he had won for himself by the motion of his body such great love for himself from us all; would we overlook the unbelievable movement of ideas and the swiftness of talents? **18** How many times I have seen Archias here, jurors,—for I will use your kindness, since you are paying attention so carefully to me in this new kind of speaking—how many times I have seen this man, although he had written not any letter, speak on the spot a large number of the best verses about those very things which were then being done, how many times he spoke the same thing which he recalled with words and sentences changed! Truly those things he had carefully and thoughtfully written, those things I have seen approved in such a way that he approached the praise of old writers. I would not cherish, I would not admire, I would not think this man should be defended by any reason? And we have learned in this way from the most respected and educated men: the studies of other things consist of education and precepts and art, that a poet has strength by his very nature and is roused by the strength of the mind and is filled by a sort of divine breath. Wherefore in his own right our Ennius called poets "holy," because they seem to be some gift of the gods and to be a reward entrusted to us.

19 Therefore, jurors, let this name of the poet, which no barbarism has ever violated, be holy among you, most civilized men. Rocks and wildernesses answer to his voice, often huge beasts are moved by his song and come to a stand; should we not be moved by the voice of poets, we who have been taught in the fine arts? The people of Colophon say that Homer is their citizen, the Chians assert that he is theirs, the people of Salamis demand it, the people of Smyrna affirm that he is their citizen; therefore they even have dedicated a shrine to him in their town, several others besides fight among themselves and argue (about this). Therefore, those (Greeks), because he was a poet, sought him even after his death, (although he was) a foreigner; are we to reject this man even as he is alive who is ours both by his own wish and by law, especially when Archias long ago brought all his zeal and all his talent in order to extol the glory and praise of the Roman people? For as a young man he dealt with the Cimbrian campaigns, and he was pleasing to that very man, Gaius Marius, who seemed rather insensitive towards these studies. **20** And there is not anyone who is so estranged from the Muses who would not easily allow a lasting proclamation of his efforts to be entrusted to verses. They say that the famous Themistocles, the greatest man in Athens, when it was asked of him what act or whose voice he listened to with the most pleasure, he had said: the voice of him by whom his own courage was most satisfactorily announced publicly. And so, that Marius likewise held dear especially Lucius Plotius, by whose talent he thought that those things which he had accomplished could be praised. **21** Indeed the great and difficult Mithridatic War carried out entirely on land and sea in a great variety (of fortune) was described by this (man, namely, Archias). These books not only made famous Lucius Lucullus, a very brave and distinguished man, but also the name of the Roman people. For the Roman people, when Lucullus was commanding, opened up the Pontus area, surrounded once by royal riches and by the very nature and region; an army of the Roman people, with the same man as leader and not with the largest band (of soldiers) routed countless troops of Armenians. It is to the credit of the

Roman people that the most friendly city of the people of Cyzicus was grabbed and saved by a plan of the same one from every royal attack and from the mouth and jaws of total war. That unbelievable naval battle at Tenedos with Lucius Lucullus fighting, always will be proclaimed and announced as ours, when after leaders had been killed, the enemy fleet was sunk; the trophies are ours, the monuments of victory are ours, ours are the triumphs. And by whose talents these things are made known, by these same men the fame of the Roman people is celebrated.

22 Our Ennius was dear to Africanus the Elder, and he is even thought to have been erected out of marble in the tomb of the Scipios. But certainly with these praises not only is it he who is praised but also the name of the Roman people is decorated. Cato, the great-grandfather of this Cato here, is raised into heaven. Great honor is added to the achievements of the Roman people. Finally, all those Maximi, Marcelli, Fulvii are adorned not without the common praise of all of us. Therefore our ancestors received into citizenship that one who had done these things, although he was a man from Rudiae (i.e., Ennius); are we to throw out this man from Heraclea from our citizenship, who was sought by many states, even established in this citizenship by our laws?

23 For if anyone thinks that a lesser benefit for glory is acquired from Greek verses rather than from Latin, he is terribly mistaken, because Greek writings are read in nearly all races, Latin writings are absolutely bound by its territories. Wherefore, if those things which we have accomplished are limited by the regions of the earth, we should want to reach glory and fame to the same place where the weapons of our men have reached glory and fame, not only because are these things great of these very peoples about whose events it is written but also of those who struggle about life for the sake of glory; this is the greatest stimulus of enduring both of dangers and of toils. **24** How many writers of his own deeds is Alexander the Great said to have had with him. But he, however, when he had stood at the tomb of Achilles in Sigeum: "O fortunate young man," he said, "who has found Homer as the announcer of your courage!" And truly: for if that famous *Iliad* had not come into being, that same tomb which had covered his body would also have buried his name. Well, what about our (Pompey) the Great here, one who has equaled fortune with his courage, did he not endow Theophanes of Mytilene, writer of his accomplishments, with citizenship in a gathering of his soldiers and those brave men of ours even though from the country, and the soldiers, moved by a kind of sweetness of glory, did they not approve that act with a great shout as if sharers of the same praise?

25 Therefore, I believe, if Archias should not be a Roman citizen by our laws, he could not make it that he be bestowed with citizenship by some general. Sulla, although he bestowed the Spaniards and Gauls, I suppose, would have refused this one (Archias) seeking citizenship. He whom we have seen in the assembly, although a bad poet from the people had supplied for him a pamphlet, which he had written an epigram on him in a little longer alternating metrical verses, immediately he ordered that a reward be granted to him from these things which he was then selling—but on this condition that he not write anything afterwards. He who considered the diligence of a bad poet worthy of some reward had not sought this man's talent and character and abundance in writing? **26** Well, would he have not sought from Quintus Metellus Pius, his most intimate friend, who bestowed many with citizenship, either by himself or through the Luculli? Especially since he wanted to be written about concerning his deeds so much that he nevertheless gave his ears even to poets born in Cordoba although uttering something coarse and foreign. For this must not be hidden which cannot be concealed but in front of us must be presented: we all are drawn by the desire for praise, and every very good person is led most greatly by glory. Those very philosophers even inscribe their name in those pamphlets which they write about scorning glory; in that very act in which they look down upon an announcement and renown, they want to be publicly declared and called by name. **27** Indeed Decimus Brutus, a very great man and general, adorned the entryways of the temples and his monuments with the poems of Accius, his dearest friend. Now truly the great Fulvius who warred with the Aetolians with Ennius as his companion, did not hesitate to vow the spoils of war to the Muses. Wherefore, in this city in which generals all but armed cultivated the name of poets and shrines of the Muses, jurors in togas should not be averse to the honor of the Muses and the security of poets.

28 And so that you may do this more freely, I now will show myself to you, jurors, I will confess to you about a certain love of mine for glory perhaps too sharp, but, however, decent. For the things which I have done in my consulship with you at the same time for the safety of this city and of the empire and for the lives of the citizens and for the universal state, this man has treated and has begun to work on in his verses. Once these were heard, because the matter seemed great and agreeable to me, I have praised him for the purpose of bringing it about. For virtue desires nothing other than a reward for its toils and dangers except this prize of praise and glory. Indeed, jurors, this having been removed, what is there which, in this so scanty and so brief a course of life, we should perform in such great times? **29** Certainly, if the mind should predict nothing into the future, and if it should limit its thoughts to those same areas by which the span of life is defined, it would neither break itself from such great efforts nor because of so many worries not be distressed by the watchful attention nor so many times would it fight about life itself. Now a certain virtue also sits inside the very good man which throughout the nights and days rouses the mind with spurs of glory and warns that a certain recollection of our name must not be dismissed in a span of life but must be made equal with all posterity. **30** Or truly do we all seem to be of such a small mind who are busy in the state and in these dangerous times of life and works, that when we have considered that there is no calm and restful spirit at the final space of time, that we will think that everything is about to die at the same time with us? If many of the great men have zealously left behind statues, death-masks, and not images of their spirits, but of their bodies, then should we not much prefer to leave behind an image of our plans and virtues pressed out and polished with our very great talents? As for me, I truly thought that in doing them, I was scattering and broadcasting into the eternal memory of the world everything which I was doing. Truly if after death this is away from my perception, or whether, as very wise men have thought, it pertains to a certain part of my mind, now indeed certainly I am delighted by a certain thought and hope.

PERORATIO
(376–397)

31 Wherefore, jurors, save a man of that honor, which you see sanctioned by both the stature of his friends and also his long relationship (with them) with talent as great as it is appropriate to be valued, which is sought by the judgments of the best men; truly his case of a sort which is affirmed with the blessing of the law, the authority of the community, the witness of Lucullus, the records of Metellus. Since these things are so, I ask from you, jurors, if there ought to be any not only human but also divine recommendation in such talent that you accept him into your trust, him who has adorned you, who has adorned your generals, who has always adorned the accomplishments of the Roman people, who, even in these recent domestic perils of yours and mine, declares that he will give an evidence of praise, and he who is in that number who always among everyone are considered and said to be blessed, that you accept him in such a way that he would seem raised by your humanity rather than violated by your bitterness.

32 Therefore, I have spoken briefly in accordance with my customary manner, jurors, those things I trust are commended to all: those things which, foreign from the forum and judicial custom, I have spoken both about the man's talent together with (his) pursuit of learning itself, those things, jurors, I hope have been welcomed by you in good part; I know for certain by him who oversees the trial.

SAMPLE ASSESSMENT QUESTIONS

1. Si quid est in me ingeni, iudices, quod sentio quam sit exiguum, aut si qua exercitatio dicendi, in qua me non infitior mediocriter esse versatum, aut si huiusce rei ratio aliqua ab optimarum artium studiis ac disciplina profecta, a qua ego nullum confiteor aetatis meae tempus abhorruisse,

5 earum rerum omnium vel in primis hic A. Licinius fructum a me repetere prope suo iure debet. Nam quoad longissime potest mens mea respicere spatium praeteriti temporis et pueritiae memoriam recordari ultimam, inde usque repetens, hunc video mihi principem et ad suscipiendam et ad ingrediendam rationem horum studiorum exstitisse. Quod si haec vox

10 huius hortatu praeceptisque conformata non nullis aliquando saluti fuit, a quo id accepimus quo ceteris opitulari et alios servare possemus, huic profecto ipsi, quantum est situm in nobis, et opem et salutem ferre debemus.

SHORT ANSWER QUESTIONS

1. Who is A. Licinius (line 5)? Give his complete Latin name.

2. In lines 1–6 (*Si . . . debet*), Cicero states that, under certain conditions, Archias should demand the benefit of all the orator's studies. Describe two of the three conditions Cicero lists.

3. When Cicero looks back to his childhood, specifically how does he say that Archias stood out?

4. Find an example of chiasmus and litotes in this section.

5. Name one figure of speech seen in this section and write out the Latin that illustrates it (excluding litotes and chiasmus).

6. In lines 9–12 (*Quod . . . debemus*), what specific training did Cicero receive from Archias and how did it influence Cicero's dealings with others?

OTHER QUESTIONS

1. Give the case and reason for that case for

   (a) *ingeni* (line 1)

   (b) *me* (line 2)

   (c) *ad suscipiendam et ad ingrediendam rationem* (lines 8–9)

   (d) *nullis . . . saluti* (line 10)

2. What is the use of the subjunctive *sit* (line 1)?

3. Write the full Latin form of the word *quid* (line 1).

2. Ac ne quis a nobis hoc ita dici forte miretur, quod alia quaedam in hoc facultas sit ingeni neque haec dicendi ratio aut disciplina, ne nos quidem huic uni studio penitus umquam dediti fuimus. Etenim omnes artes quae ad humanitatem pertinent habent quoddam commune vinculum et quasi
5   cognatione quadam inter se continentur.

SHORT ANSWER QUESTION

1. What is Cicero's comment about the arts that pertain to civilization?

OTHER QUESTIONS

1. Give the mood and syntax for

    (a) *dici* (line 1)

    (b) *miretur* (line 1)

    (c) *sit* (line 2)

2. What tone is expressed by Cicero in line 2 with the phrase *ne nos quidem*?

3. Sed ne cui vestrum mirum esse videatur me in quaestione legitima et in
iudicio publico, cum res agatur apud praetorem populi Romani, lectissimum
virum, et apud severissimos iudices, tanto conventu hominum ac frequentia,
hoc uti genere dicendi, quod non modo a consuetudine iudiciorum, verum

5   etiam a forensi sermone abhorreat, quaeso a vobis ut in hac causa mihi
detis hanc veniam accommodatam huic reo, vobis, quemadmodum
spero, non molestam, ut me pro summo poeta atque eruditissimo homine
dicentem hoc concursu hominum litteratissimorum, hac vestra humanitate,
hoc denique praetore exercente iudicium, patiamini de studiis humanitatis

10   ac litterarum paulo loqui liberius, et in eius modi persona quae propter
otium ac studium minime in iudiciis periculisque tractata est uti prope
novo quodam et inusitato genere dicendi.

SHORT ANSWER QUESTIONS

1. In lines 1–5 (*Sed . . . abhorreat*), why might the jury wonder at Cicero's type of speaking in this court case?

2. Cicero flatters several individuals and groups here. Give two examples, citing the Latin and English of such comments.

3. What two figures of speech are seen in lines 8–9 (*hoc concursu . . . iudicium*), and how are they representative of Ciceronian style?

4. Give an example of hendiadys in this section.

5. How has Archias spent his time instead of risking the hazards of the courtroom (lines 10–11)?

6. Why do you think Cicero has included a number of superlatives in this section? What effect does this create?

OTHER QUESTIONS

1. Give the case and reason for that case for

    (a) *vestrum* (line 1)

    (b) *genere* (line 4)

2. Give the mood and usage for

    (a) *videatur* (line 1)

    (b) *detis* (line 6)

    (c) *loqui* (line 10)

3. What part of speech is *liberius* (line 10)?

Essay Question

To defend Archias successfully, Cicero decided upon a less customary courtroom procedure. In a well-written essay, describe his new approach and include how Cicero approaches the jury, requests the exception he wants, and defends his request. What Ciceronian elements (e.g., rhetorical devices, word placement) are evident and how do they help his case? Be sure to include the Latin (translated or paraphrased into English) that supports your ideas.

4. Quod si mihi a vobis tribui concedique sentiam, perficiam profecto
ut hunc A. Licinium non modo non segregandum, cum sit civis,
a numero civium verum etiam, si non esset, putetis asciscendum fuisse.

5   Nam, ut primum ex pueris excessit Archias atque ab eis artibus quibus
aetas puerilis ad humanitatem informari solet, se ad scribendi studium
contulit. Primum Antiochiae—nam ibi natus est loco nobili—celebri quondam
urbe et copiosa atque eruditissimis hominibus liberalissimisque studiis
adfluenti, celeriter antecellere omnibus ingeni gloria coepit. Post
in ceteris Asiae partibus cunctaque Graecia sic eius adventus celebrabantur
10   ut famam ingeni exspectatio hominis, exspectationem ipsius adventus
admiratioque superaret.

SHORT ANSWER QUESTIONS

1. Translate lines 1–3 (*Quod . . . fuisse*).

2. To what did Archias apply himself after boyhood (lines 4–6)? Was he successful?

3. How does Cicero describe the city of Antioch when Archias lived there?

4. In lines 8–11 (*Post . . . superaret*), what does Cicero tell us about the people's reactions to Archias in Asia and Greece?

5. List examples of and comment on Cicero's use of superlatives in this section.

6. Lines 1–3 of this section marks the end of what element of a formal oration? In the second part of a formal speech called the *narratio* (*Nam, ut primum . . .*), what does the speaker do?

OTHER QUESTIONS

1. Give the case and reason for that case for

   (a)   *Antiochiae* (line 6)

   (b)   *loco* (line 6)

   (c)   *omnibus* (line 8)

   (d)   *gloria* (line 8)

   (e)   *ipsius* (line 10)

5. Erat Italia tum plena Graecarum artium ac disciplinarum, studiaque
haec et in Latio vehementius tum colebantur quam nunc isdem in oppidis,
et hic Romae propter tranquillitatem rei publicae non neglegebantur. Itaque
hunc et Tarentini et Locrenses et Regini et Neapolitani civitate ceterisque
5   praemiis donarunt, et omnes qui aliquid de ingeniis poterant iudicare
cognitione atque hospitio dignum existimarunt. Hac tanta celebritate
famae cum esset iam absentibus notus, Romam venit Mario consule et
Catulo. Nactus est primum consules eos quorum alter res ad scribendum
maximas, alter cum res gestas tum etiam studium atque auris adhibere
10   posset. Statim Luculli, cum praetextatus etiam tum Archias esset, eum
domum suam receperunt. Dedit etiam hoc non solum lumen ingeni ac litterarum,
verum etiam naturae atque virtutis ut domus, quae huius adulescentiae
prima favit, eadem esset familiarissima senectuti.

Short Answer Questions

1. During the time period in this section, how receptive were Latium and Rome itself to Greek arts and studies?

2. How did the peoples of southern Italy respond to the abilities of Archias (lines 3–6)?

3. When Archias came to Rome, what did each of the two consuls, Marius and Catulus, offer to his literary talents (lines 8–10)?

4. What part did the house of the Luculli play in the life of Archias (lines 10–13)?

Other Questions

1. Give the case and reason for that case for

    (a) *cognitione et hospitio* (line 6)

    (b) *Mario consule et Catulo* (lines 7–8)

    (c) *adulescentiae* (line 12)

2. Why is *esset* (line 10) in the subjunctive?

Essay Question

For Cicero, proving the citizenship of Archias was more than citing documents. Using Latin (with English translation/paraphrase) to support your answer, write an essay describing how, in this section, Cicero emphasizes the connection of the poet to Italy and Rome. How well did he fit in? What factors affected his status in the cultural and social life of the city? Provide specific examples. Include at least one figure of speech in your essay and discuss how it enhances this passage.

6. Erat temporibus illis iucundus Q. Metello, illi Numidico, et eius
Pio filio, audiebatur a M. Aemilio, vivebat cum Q. Catulo et patre et
filio, a L. Crasso colebatur. Lucullos vero et Drusum et Octavios et
Catonem et totam Hortensiorum domum devinctam consuetudine cum

5   teneret, adficiebatur summo honore, quod eum non solum colebant,
qui aliquid percipere atque audire studebant, verum etiam si qui forte
simulabant. Interim satis longo intervallo, cum esset cum M. Lucullo
in Siciliam profectus et cum ex ea provincia cum eodem Lucullo
decederet, venit Heracleam. Quae cum esset civitas aequissimo iure

10   ac foedere, ascribi se in eam civitatem voluit idque, cum ipse per se
dignus putaretur, tum auctoritate et gratia Luculli ab Heracliensibus
impetravit.

SHORT ANSWER QUESTIONS

1. In lines 1–7 Cicero mentions Archias' acceptance by several notable Romans. Select three and describe how each showed his approval of the poet.

2. What relationship did the city of Heraclea have with Rome (lines 9–10)? Why did Archias want to be enrolled as a citizen there?

3. How did Archias obtain citizenship in Heraclea (lines 11–12)?

OTHER QUESTIONS

1. Give the case and reason for that case for

    (a) *Metello* (line 1)

    (b) *idque* (line 10)

2. Identify the subject of *esset* (line 7).

7. Data est civitas Silvani lege et Carbonis: Sɪ QUI FOEDERATIS CIVITATIBUS
ASCRIPTI FUISSENT, SI TUM CUM LEX FEREBATUR IN ITALIA DOMICILIUM HABUISSENT
ET SI SEXAGINTA DIEBUS APUD PRAETOREM ESSENT PROFESSI. Cum hic domicilium
Romae multos iam annos haberet, professus est apud praetorem Q. Metel-
5   lum, familiarissimum suum.

SHORT ANSWER QUESTIONS

1.   According to the law of Silvanus and Carbo, what two conditions had to be met for citizenship in
     states allied to Rome (lines 1–3)?

2.   Briefly explain how Archias fulfilled these requirements (lines 3–5).

OTHER QUESTIONS

1.   What tense and mood are the verbs *fuissent* and *habuissent* (line 2)?

2.   What is the case and reason for that case for *diebus* (line 3)?

3.   What is the best translation for *Cum* (line 3)?

4.   To whom does *suum* (line 5) refer?

8. Si nihil aliud nisi de civitate ac lege dicimus, nihil dico amplius:
causa dicta est. Quid enim horum informari, Gratti, potest?
Heracleaene esse tum ascriptum negabis? Adest vir summa
auctoritate et religione et fide, M. Lucullus, qui se non opinari

5   sed scire, non audisse sed vidisse, non interfuisse sed egisse dicit.
Adsunt Heraclienses legati, nobilissimi homines, huius iudici causa
cum mandatis et cum publico testimonio venerunt, qui hunc ascriptum
Heracleae esse dicunt. Hic tu tabulas desideras Hercliensium publicas,
quas Italico bello incenso tabulario interisse scimus omnes? Est

10   ridiculum ad ea quae habemus nihil dicere, quaerere quae habere
non possumus, et de hominum memoria tacere, litterarum memoriam
flagitare et, cum habeas amplissimi viri religionem, integerrimi municipi
ius iurandum fidemque, ea quae depravari nullo modo possunt repudiare,
tabulas quas idem dicis solere corrumpi desiderare.

SHORT ANSWER QUESTIONS

1. According to Cicero, how did M. Lucullus help prove the citizenship of Archias (lines 3–5)?

2. What weight did the Heraclean envoys provide (lines 6–8)? How useful were the public records of Heraclea (lines 8–9)?

3. At the end of this section, Cicero criticizes Grattius' demand for more proof as *ridiculum*. Give three examples from Cicero's list of his opponent's demands.

4. Section 8 begins the third part of a classical speech. What is this element called and what is its purpose?

OTHER QUESTIONS

1. Give the case and reason for that case for

   (a)   *Gratti* (line 2)

   (b)   *Heracleae* (line 3)

   (c)   *auctoritate et religione et fide* (line 4)

   (d)   *se* (line 4)

   (e)   *huius iudici* (line 6)

   (f)   *quas* (line 9)

   (g)   *quae* (line 10)

2. Give the mood and identify the usage for

   (a)   *opinari* (line 4)

   (b)   *habeas* (line 12)

9. An domicilium Romae non habuit is qui tot annis ante civitatem datam sedem omnium rerum ac fortunarum suarum Romae conlocavit? An non est professus? Immo vero eis tabulis professus quae solae ex illa professione conlegioque praetorum obtinent publicarum
5   tabularum auctoritatem. Nam, cum Appi tabulae neglegentius adservatae dicerentur, Gabini, quam diu incolumis fuit, levitas, post damnationem calamitas omnem tabularum fidem resignasset, Metellus, homo sanctissimus modestissimusque omnium, tanta diligentia fuit ut ad L. Lentulum praetorem et ad iudices venerit
10   et unius nominis litura se commotum esse dixerit. His igitur in tabulis nullam lituram in nomine A. Licini videtis.

SHORT ANSWER QUESTIONS

1. Comment on the reliability of the public records mentioned above:

    (a)   in which Archias was registered (lines 3–5)

    (b)   of Appius (lines 5–6)

    (c)   of Gabinius (lines 6–7)

2. How did Metellus show exemplary behavior (lines 8–10)?

OTHER QUESTIONS

1. Give the case and the reason for that case for

    (a)   *Romae* (line 1)

    (b)   *levitas* (line 6)

    (c)   *se* (line 10)

2. What is the tense of *resignasset* (line 7)? Write the full Latin form of this verb.

10. Quae cum ita sint, quid est quod de eius civitate dubitetis,
praesertim cum aliis quoque in civitatibus fuerit ascriptus? Etenim
cum mediocribus multis et aut nulla aut humili aliqua arte praeditis
gratuito civitatem in Graecia homines impertiebant, Reginos credo
5   aut Locrensis aut Neapolitanos aut Tarentinos, quod scaenicis
artificibus largiri solebant, id huic summa ingeni praedito gloria
noluisse! Quid? Cum ceteri non modo post civitatem datam sed
etiam post legem Papiam aliquo modo in eorum municipiorum tabulas
inrepserunt, hic qui ne utitur quidem illis in quibus est scriptus, quod
10   semper se Heracliensem esse voluit, reicietur?

SHORT ANSWER QUESTIONS

1. Comment on how Cicero contrasts the situation of Archias concerning citizenship when compared to

    (a) persons in Magna Graecia (lines 2–4)

    (b) actors (lines 4–6)

    (c) others after the *Lex Papia* was passed (lines 7–10)

2. Where do we see Cicero's use of irony in this passage? Cite the Latin used and briefly explain its application here.

OTHER QUESTIONS

1. What is the best translation for *cum* (line 1)?

2. To whom or what does *huic* (line 6) refer?

3. What is the tense of the verb *reicietur* (line 10)?

11. Census nostros requiris. Scilicet! Est enim obscurum proximis censoribus hunc cum clarissimo imperatore L. Lucullo apud exercitum fuisse, superioribus cum eodem quaestore fuisse in Asia, primis Iulio et Crasso nullam populi partem esse censam. Sed, quoniam census

5   non ius civitatis confirmat ac tantum modo indicat eum, qui sit census, ita se iam tum gessisse pro cive, eis temporibus is quem tu criminaris ne ipsius quidem iudicio in civium Romanorum iure esse versatum et testamentum saepe fecit nostris legibus, et adiit hereditates civium Romanorum, et in beneficiis ad aerarium delatus est a L. Lucullo

10   pro consule. Quaere argumenta, si quae potes; numquam enim hic neque suo neque amicorum iudicio revincetur.

SHORT ANSWER QUESTIONS

1. How does Cicero explain why Archias has not been on the last three census lists of citizens (lines 1–3)?

2. Using the information Cicero gives,

    (a) what do census lists show regarding citizenship (lines 4–6)?

    (b) specifically how does Archias, therefore, qualify for citizenship (lines 7–10)?

3. What tone is expressed by Cicero through his use of *Scilicet* (line 1), and how does he continue this tone in the next sentence?

OTHER QUESTIONS

1. Give the mood and usage for

    (a) *fuisse* (line 3)

    (b) *sit* (line 5)

    (c) *criminaris* (line 6)

    (d) *Quaere* (line 10)

2. To whom does *is* (line 6) refer?

12. Quaeres a nobis, Gratti, cur tanto opere hoc homine delectemur.
Quia suppeditat nobis ubi et animus ex hoc forensi strepitu reficiatur
et aures convicio defessae conquiescant. An tu existimas aut suppetere
nobis posse quod cotidie dicamus in tanta varietate rerum, nisi animos

5   nostros doctrina excolamus, aut ferre animos tantam posse contentionem,
nisi eos doctrina eadem relaxemus? Ego vero fateor me his studiis esse
deditum. Ceteros pudeat, si qui ita se litteris abdiderunt ut nihil possint
ex eis neque ad communem adferre fructum neque in aspectum lucemque
proferre; me autem quid pudeat qui tot annos ita vivo, iudices, ut a nullius

10   umquam me tempore aut commodo aut otium meum abstraxerit aut
voluptas avocarit aut denique somnus retardarit?

SHORT ANSWER QUESTIONS

1. Translate as literally as you can into good English lines 1–6 (*Quaeres . . . relaxemus?*)

2. In lines 6–11 (*Ego . . . retardarit*), Cicero criticizes certain kinds of scholars. In a short essay, describe what they do wrong and why he is able to exclude himself from this group.

3. What figure of speech is seen in the phrase *in aspectum lucemque* (line 8)?

4. The fourth part of an ancient speech begins with this section. What is this part of an oration called and what is its function?

OTHER QUESTIONS

1. Give the literal and conversational meaning of *tanto opere* (line 1).

2. Give the mood and usage for

   (a) *pudeat* (line 7)

   (b) *possint* (line 7)

   (c) *adferre* (line 8)

3. What is the tense of the verbs *avocarit* and *retardarit* (line 11)? Write their full Latin forms.

13. Quare quis tandem me reprehendat, aut quis mihi iure suscenseat,
si, quantum ceteris ad suas res obeundas, quantum ad festos dies ludorum
celebrandos, quantum ad alias voluptates et ad ipsam requiem animi et
corporis conceditur temporum, quantum alii tribuunt tempestivis
5   conviviis, quantum denique alveolo, quantum pilae, tantum mihi egomet
ad haec studia recolenda sumpsero? Atque id eo mihi concedendum est
magis quod ex his studiis haec quoque crescit oratio et facultas quae,
quantacumque est in me, numquam amicorum periculis defuit. Quae
si cui levior videtur, illa quidem certe quae summa sunt ex quo fonte
10   hauriam sentio.

SHORT ANSWER QUESTIONS

1. What distinctions does Cicero draw between his activities and those of others in Roman society (lines 1–6)?

2. What talent has Cicero developed as a result of his activities and how has it benefited his friends (lines 6–8)?

3. Identify the anaphora in lines 1–6 and discuss briefly the effect it has on the overall point Cicero is trying to make in this section.

4. What figure of speech is seen in the phrase *oratio et facultas* (line 7)?

5. What specific words used by Cicero create a somewhat self-congratulatory tone in this passage?

OTHER QUESTIONS

1. Give the mood and usage for *reprehendat* (line 1).

2. Write the Latin and English for a gerundive of purpose found in this section.

3. Give the case and reason for that case for

    (a) *animi* (line 3)

    (b) *mihi* (line 6)

    (c) *periculis* (line 8)

    (d) *Quae* (line 8)

14. Nam nisi multorum praeceptis multisque litteris mihi ab
adulescentia suasissem nihil esse in vita magno opere expetendum nisi
laudem atque honestatem, in ea autem persequenda omnis cruciatus corporis,
omnia pericula mortis atque exsili parvi esse ducenda, numquam me pro

5   salute vestra in tot ac tantas dimicationes atque in hos profligatorum
hominum cotidianos impetus obiecissem. Sed pleni omnes sunt libri, plenae
sapientium voces, plena exemplorum vetustas; quae iacerent in tenebris
omnia, nisi litterarum lumen accederet. Quam multas nobis imagines non
solum ad intuendum verum etiam ad imitandum fortissimorum virorum

10   expressas scriptores et Graeci et Latini reliquerunt! Quas ego mihi
semper in administranda re publica proponens animum et mentem meam
ipsa cogitatione hominum excellentium conformabam.

SHORT ANSWER QUESTIONS

1. In lines 1–3, what does Cicero say he has learned from studying literature that are the highest goals in life?

2. To what specific historical event does Cicero refer in lines 4–6 (*numquam . . . obiecissem*)?

3. Identify the figure of speech in lines 6–7 and discuss how it adds to the impact of the passage.

4. What or who provide guidance in conducting one's life? How? How has Cicero specifically used these resources?

OTHER QUESTIONS

1. Give the mood and usage for

    (a) *suasissem* (line 2)

2. What is the case and reason for that case for:

    (b) *omnis* (line 3)

    (c) *sapientium* (line 7)

3. What does *proponens* (line 11) modify?

15. Quaeret quispiam: "Quid? Illi ipsi summi viri, quorum virtutes litteris proditae sunt, istane doctrina quam tu effers laudibus eruditi fuerunt?" Difficile est hoc de omnibus confirmare, sed tamen est certum quid respondeam. Ego multos homines excellenti animo ac virtute

5 fuisse et sine doctrina, naturae ipsius habitu prope divino per se ipsos et moderatos et gravis exstitisse fateor; etiam illud adiungo: saepius ad laudem atque virtutem naturam sine doctrina quam sine natura valuisse doctrinam. Atque idem ego hoc contendo: cum ad naturam eximiam et inlustrem accesserit ratio quaedam conformatioque doctrinae,

10 tum illud nescioquid praeclarum ac singulare solere exsistere.

Short Answer Questions

1. In lines 4–6 (*Ego . . . fateor*), what does Cicero admit about those who have not received the type of learning he praises? What figure of speech does he use (line 4)?

2. What are Cicero's comments about character and learning (lines 6–8)?

3. What occurs when training and natural brilliance are joined (lines 8–10)?

Other Questions

1. What is the mood and usage for

    (a) *respondeam* (line 4)

    (b) *exstitisse* (line 6)

    (c) *accesserit* (line 9)

2. What is the case and reason for that case for

    (a) *excellenti animo ac virtute* (line 4)

    (b) *illud* (line 6)

3. What is the translation of *quam* (line 7)?

16. Ex hoc esse hunc numero quem patres nostri viderunt, divinum hominem, Africanum, ex hoc C. Laelium, L. Furium, moderatissimos homines et continentissimos, ex hoc fortissimum virum et illis temporibus doctissimum, M. Catonem illum senem. Qui profecto si nihil ad
5 percipiendam colendamque virtutem litteris adiuvarentur, numquam se ad earum studium contulissent. Quod si non hic tantus fructus ostenderetur, et si ex his studiis delectatio sola peteretur, tamen, ut opinor, hanc animi remissionem humanissimam ac liberalissimam iudicaretis. Nam ceterae neque temporum sunt neque aetatum omnium
10 neque locorum; at haec studia adulescentiam acuunt, senectutem oblectant, secundas res ornant, adversis perfugium ac solacium praebent, delectant domi, non impediunt foris, pernoctant nobiscum, peregrinantur, rusticantur.

SHORT ANSWER QUESTIONS

1. According to Cicero, why did notable Romans like Scipio Africanus and Marcus Cato the Elder pursue the study of literature (lines 4–6)?

2. How do literary studies surpass other forms of relaxation and enjoyment? Give three examples, citing the Latin and English (lines 9–13).

3. What is the effect of Cicero's use of superlatives in this section? Use the Latin and English in your discussion.

OTHER QUESTIONS

1. Give the mood and usage for *adiuvarentur* (line 5).

2. Give the case and reason for that case for

    (a) *adversis* (line 11)

    (b) *domi* (line 12)

3. Keeping the same case, give the comparative of the adjective *fortissimum* (line 3).

17. Quod si ipsi haec neque attingere neque sensu nostro gustare
possemus, tamen ea mirari deberemus, etiam cum in aliis videremus.
Quis nostrum tam animo agresti ac duro fuit ut Rosci morte nuper
non commoveretur? qui cum esset senex mortuus, tamen propter
5   excellentem artem ac venustatem videbatur omnino mori non
debuisse. Ergo ille corporis motu tantum amorem sibi conciliarat
a nobis omnibus; nos animorum incredibilis motus celeritatemque
ingeniorum neglegemus?

Short Answer Questions

1. How does Cicero use the career of Roscius to strengthen his argument for the talents of Archias (lines 4–7)?

2. Identify and give the Latin for the figure of speech in lines 6–8 (*Ergo . . . neglegemus*).

Other Questions

1. Give the tense, mood, and usage for

    (a) *possemus* (line 2)

    (b) *mori* (line 5)

2. Give the case and reason for that case for

    (a) *nostrum* (line 3)

    (b) *animo agresti ac duro* (line 3)

    (c) *incredibilis* (line 7)

18. Quotiens ego hunc Archiam vidi, iudices—utar enim vestra
benignitate, quoniam me in hoc novo genere dicendi tam diligenter
atteneditis—quotiens ego hunc vidi, cum litteram scripsisset nullam,
magnum numerum optimorum versuum de eis ipsis rebus quae tum

5   agerentur dicere ex tempore, quotiens revocatum eandem rem dicere
commutatis verbis atque sententiis! Quae vero accurate cogitateque
scripsisset, ea sic vidi probari ut ad veterum scriptorum laudem perveniret.
Hunc ego non diligam, non admirer, non omni ratione defendendum putem?
Atque sic a summis hominibus eruditissimisque accepimus, ceterarum

10   rerum studia ex doctrina et praeceptis et arte constare, poetam natura
ipsa valere et mentis viribus excitari et quasi divino quodam spiritu inflari.
Quare suo iure noster ille Ennius "sanctos" appellat poetas, quod quasi
deorum aliquo dono atque munere commendati nobis esse videantur.

Short Answer Questions

1. In lines 1–6 (*Quotiens . . . sententiis*) of this section, what specific talent of Archias does Cicero praise? Give the Latin and English.

2. How does Cicero describe the writings of Archias (line 6)? How successful were these writings?

3. Find an example of a tricolon crescens in this section and provide the Latin.

4. How have the most learned men distinguished the art of writing poetry from other studies? Who was Ennius and why did he call poets *sanctos* (line 12)?

Other Questions

1. What is the tense, mood, voice, and translation for *utar* (line 1)?

2. What is the form of *dicendi* (line 2)?

3. To what or whom does *hunc* (line 3) refer?

4. What is the case of *revocatum* (line 5) and what does it modify?

5. What part of speech are the words *accurate cogitateque* (line 6)

6. Why are *diligam, non admirer, non . . . putem* (line 8) in the subjunctive? Translate each one.

7. Give the mood and usage for *constare, valere, excitari, inflari* (lines 10–11).

Essay Question

In defending Archias, Cicero also extolled the study of the liberal arts. In a well-written essay, show how in this section Cicero builds his argument from the specific to the general in his defense of poetry and literature. What rhetorical devices do you think helped his presentation? Why do you think he ended this section in this way?

19. Sit igitur, iudices, sanctum apud vos, humanissimos homines,
hoc poetae nomen quod nulla umquam barbaria violavit. Saxa atque
solitudines voci respondent, bestiae saepe immanes cantu flectuntur
atque consistunt; nos instituti rebus optimis non poetarum voce moveamur?

5   Homerum Colophonii civem esse dicunt suum, Chii suum vindicant,
Salaminii repetunt, Smyrnaei vero suum esse confirmant itaque etiam
delubrum eius in oppido dedicaverunt, permulti alii praeterea pugnant
inter se atque contendunt. Ergo illi alienum, quia poeta fuit, post mortem
etiam expetunt; nos hunc vivum qui et voluntate et legibus noster est

10   repudiamus, praesertim cum omne olim studium atque omne ingenium
contulerit Archias ad populi Romani gloriam laudemque celebrandam?
Nam et Cimbricas res adulescens attigit et ipsi illi C. Mario qui durior
ad haec studia videbatur iucundus fuit.

SHORT ANSWER QUESTIONS

1. In this section, Cicero exalts the poet in society. In what ways have both men and nature responded to the art of the poet (lines 2–4)?

2. Why are the peoples of Colophon, Chios, Salamis, and Smyrna mentioned here (lines 5–7)?

3. Why does Cicero nearly scold the jury for its possible mistreatment of Archias (lines 8–10)?

4. What has Archias done for the Roman people (lines 10–12)? What is the role of Marius in this discussion (lines 12–13)?

OTHER QUESTIONS

1. Give the the use of the subjunctive and translate each.

   (a) *Sit* (line 1)

   (b) *moveamur* (line 4)

   (c) *repudiamus* (line 10)

2. Give the case and reason for that case for

   (a) *saxa* (line 2)

   (b) *voci* (line 3)

   (c) *civem* (line 5)

3. Translate *suum* (line 5). To whom or what does it refer?

4. Translate *hunc* (line 9). To whom or what does it refer?

20. Neque enim quisquam est tam aversus a Musis qui non mandari versibus aeternum suorum laborum praeconium facile patiatur. Themistoclem illum, summum Athenis virum, dixisse aiunt, cum ex eo quaereretur quod acroama aut cuius vocem libentissime audiret: eius
5   a quo sua virtus optime praedicaretur. Itaque ille Marius item eximie L. Plotium dilexit, cuius ingenio putabat ea quae gesserat posse celebrari.

SHORT ANSWER QUESTIONS

1. What comparison does Cicero make between the Athenian Themistocles and the Roman Marius, although they are separated by nearly four hundred years of history? Give the Latin and English.

2. Translate the phrase *aversus a Musis* (line 1) and discuss briefly how it relates to Cicero's purpose here.

3. Identify *L. Plotium* (line 6).

OTHER QUESTIONS

1. What is the use for each subjunctive?

    (a) *patiatur* (line 2)

    (b) *quaereretur* (line 4)

    (c) *praedicaretur* (line 5)

2. Give the gender, number, case, and reason for that case for *ea* (line 6).

3. Give the usage for these infinitives.

    (a) *dixisse* (line 3)

    (b) *posse* (line 6)

    (c) *celebrari* (line 7)

21. Mithridaticum vero bellum magnum atque difficile et in multa varietate terra marique versatum totum ab hoc expressum est; qui libri non modo L. Lucullum, fortissimum et clarissimum virum, verum etiam populi Romani nomen inlustrant. Populus enim Romanus aperuit Lucullo imperante Pontum

5   et regiis quondam opibus et ipsa natura et regione vallatum, populi Romani exercitus eodem duce non maxima manu innumerabilis Armeniorum copias fudit, populi Romani laus est urbem amicissimam Cyzicenorum eiusdem consilio ex omni impetu regio atque totius belli ore ac faucibus ereptam esse atque servatam. Nostra semper feretur et praedicabitur

10   L. Lucullo dimicante, cum interfectis ducibus depressa hostium classis est, incredibilis apud Tenedum pugna illa navalis, nostra sunt tropaea, nostra monumenta, nostri triumphi. Quae quorum ingeniis efferuntur, ab eis populi Romani fama celebratur.

SHORT ANSWER QUESTIONS

1. Why was the Mithridatic war difficult (lines 1–2)?

2. How did Archias glorify the Roman people in his writings about the achievements of Lucius Lucullus (lines 11–13)?

3. What Latin words represent an example of hendiadys in line 5?

4. In addition to polyptoton what figure of speech is seen in the words *Nostra . . . nostra . . . nostra . . . nostri* (lines 10–13)? How does it enhance Cicero's message in this section?

OTHER QUESTIONS

1. To whom or what does *hoc* (line 2) refer?

2. Give the case and syntax for

    (a)   *Lucullo imperante* (line 4)

    (b)   *ipsa natura et regione* (line 5)

    (c)   *interfectis ducibus* (line 10)

22. Carus fuit Africano superiori noster Ennius, itaque etiam in
sepulcro Scipionum putatur is esse constitutus ex marmore. At eis
laudibus certe non solum ipse qui laudatur sed etiam populi Romani
nomen ornatur. In caelum huius proavus Cato tollitur; magnus honos
5   populi Romani rebus adiungitur. Omnes denique illi Maximi, Marcelli,
Fulvii non sine communi omnium nostrum laude decorantur. Ergo illum
qui haec fecerat, Rudinum hominem, maiores nostri in civitatem receperunt;
nos hunc Heracliensem, multis civitatibus expetitum, in hac autem legibus
constitutum, de nostra civitate eiciamus?

SHORT ANSWER QUESTIONS

1. At the opening of this section, Cicero comments on the writings of Ennius.

   (a) How was Ennius treated by Scipio the Elder (lines 1–2)?

   (b) How did the poetry of Ennius go beyond the mere recording of events (lines 2–5)?

2. Who is *Rudinum hominem* (line 7)? *hunc Heracliensem* (line 8)? How did their treatment by the Roman state differ?

OTHER QUESTIONS

1. Give the case and reason for that case for

   (a) *superiori* (line 1)

   (b) *Scipionum* (line 2)

   (c) *communi* (line 6)

   (d) *haec* (line 7)

2. To whom or what does *huius* (line 4) refer?

3. Translate the verb *eiciamus* (line 9).

23. Nam si quis minorem gloriae fructum putat ex Graecis versibus percipi
quam ex Latinis, vehementer errat, propterea quod Graeca leguntur in
omnibus fere gentibus, Latina suis finibus exiguis sane continentur. Quare, si
res eae quas gessimus orbis terrae regionibus definiuntur, cupere debemus,

5   quo hominum nostrorum tela pervenerint, eodem gloriam famamque
penetrare, quod cum ipsis populis de quorum rebus scribitur haec ampla
sunt, tum eis certe qui de vita gloriae causa dimicant hoc maximum et periculorum
incitamentum est et laborum.

Short Answer Questions

1. What is the unexpressed noun which *Graeca* (line 2) and *Latina* (line 3) modify?

2. Why does Cicero see no problem if Roman achievements are glorified by a poet writing in Greek rather than Latin (lines 2–3)?

3. What other purpose might such writings have besides glorifying deeds of nations (lines 4–8)?

Other Questions

1. What is the full Latin form of *quis* (line 1)? Translate the first three words of this sentence.

2. Give the mood and usage and translate *percipi* (line 1).

3. Give the meaning of *quo* (line 5) and *eodem* (line 5).

24. Quam multos scriptores rerum suarum magnus ille Alexander
secum habuisse dicitur. Atque is tamen, cum in Sigeo ad Achillis tumulum
astitisset: "O fortunate," inquit "adulescens, qui tuae virtutis Homerum
praeconem inveneris!" Et vere: nam nisi Ilias illa exstitisset, idem
5   tumulus qui corpus eius contexerat nomen etiam obruisset. Quid?
Noster hic Magnus qui cum virtute fortunam adaequavit, nonne
Theophanem Mytilenaeum, scriptorem rerum suarum, in contione
militum civitate donavit, et nostri illi fortes viri, sed rustici ac milites,
dulcedine quadam gloriae commoti quasi participes eiusdem laudis
10   magno illud clamore approbaverunt?

Short Answer Questions

1. Comment on Cicero's word placement in describing Alexander in line 1.

2. When he stood at the tomb of Achilles, why did Alexander the Great call the hero "fortunate" (lines 3–4)? Why did Cicero agree with him (lines 4–5)?

3. Who was Theophanes (line 7)? How did Pompey reward him and why were his soldiers so favorable to this reward (lines 7–10)?

4. Find and give the Latin for a chiasmus in line 9.

Other Questions

1. Translate the first word of the section.

2. Give the mood, usage, and translation for

   (a) *astitisset* (line 3)

   (b) *inveneris* (line 4)

   (c) *exstitisset* (line 4)

   (d) *obruisset* (line 5)

3. Give the case, reason for that case, and reference for

   (a) *fortunate* (line 3)

   (b) *eius* (line 5)

   (c) *suarum* (line 7)

   (d) *illud* (line 10)

25. Itaque, credo, si civis Romanus Archias legibus non esset, ut ab aliquo imperatore civitate donaretur perficere non potuit. Sulla cum Hispanos et Gallos donaret, credo, hunc petentem repudiasset. Quem nos in contione vidimus, cum ei libellum malus poeta de populo subiecisset, quod
5   epigramma in eum fecisset tantum modo alternis versibus longiusculis, statim ex eis rebus, quas tum vendebat, iubere ei praemium tribui—sed ea condicione ne quid postea scriberet. Qui sedulitatem mali poetae duxerit aliquo tamen praemio dignam, huius ingenium et virtutem in scribendo et copiam non expetisset?

Short Answer Questions

1. Is Cicero's use of *credo* (lines 1 and 3) genuine or sarcastic? Discuss briefly.

2. Cicero cites an episode in which Sulla rewarded a bad poet.

    (a)   What was the condition attached to the reward (line7)?

    (b)   Why might Sulla have sought out Archias instead (lines 7–9)?

    (c)   *Alternis versibus longiusculis* (lines 5–6) refers to what poetic meter?

Other Questions

1. Give the mood and usage for

    (a)   *esset* (line 1)

    (b)   *repudiasset* (line 3)

2. To whom does each refer?

    (a)   *hunc* (line 3)

    (b)   *ei* (line 4)

    (c)   *Qui* (line 7)

    (d)   *huius* (line 8)

Essay Question

In sections 10 (below) and 25 (cf. p. 56), Cicero describes the granting of citizenship to recipients seemingly "less worthy" than Archias. Contrast these situations with that of Archias. Why does he seem "more worthy" of citizenship than the others? What tone is prevalent in both examples and why?

> **10.** Quae cum ita sint, quid est quod de eius civitate dubitetis,
> praesertim cum aliis quoque in civitatibus fuerit ascriptus? Etenim
> cum mediocribus multis et aut nulla aut humili aliqua arte praeditis
> gratuito civitatem in Graecia homines impertiebant, Reginos credo
> 5   aut Locrensis aut Neapolitanos aut Tarentinos, quod scaenicis
> artificibus largiri solebant, id huic summa ingeni praedito gloria
> noluisse! Quid? Cum ceteri non modo post civitatem datam sed
> etiam post legem Papiam aliquo modo in eorum municipiorum tabulas
> inrepserunt, hic qui ne utitur quidem illis in quibus est scriptus, quod
> 10   semper se Heracliensem esse voluit, reicietur?

26. Quid? a Q. Metello Pio, familiarissimo suo, qui civitate multos
donavit, neque per se neque per Lucullos impetravisset? qui praesertim
usque eo de suis rebus scribi cuperet ut etiam Cordubae natis poetis
pingue quiddam sonantibus atque peregrinum tamen auris suas dederet.

5   Neque enim est hoc dissimulandum quod obscurari non potest, sed prae
nobis ferendum: trahimur omnes studio laudis, et optimus quisque
maxime gloria ducitur. Ipsi illi philosophi etiam in eis libellis quos
de contemnenda gloria scribunt nomen suum inscribunt; in eo ipso
in quo praedicationem nobilitatemque despiciunt praedicari de se ac

10   nominari volunt.

SHORT ANSWER QUESTIONS

1. Why might Q. Metellus Pius have been of some help to Archias in obtaining citizenship (lines 1–2)?

2. To what lengths had Marcellus gone to be glorified in verse (lines 2–4)?

3. Translate lines 5–7 (*Neque . . . ducitur*) as literally as you can into good English.

4. Why might certain philosophers seem hypocritical about being glorified?

OTHER QUESTIONS

1. Give the case, reason for that case, and a translation for *familiarissimo suo* (line 1).

2. To whom does *se* (line 2) refer?

3. What conjunction seems to be missing from the opening of the sentence *qui praesertim* (line 2)?

4. Give the case and reason for that case for

    (a) *Cordubae* (line 3)

    (b) *pingue* (line 4)

    (c) *auris* (line 4)

    (d) *se* (line 9) To what or whom does this pronoun refer?

27. Decimus quidem Brutus, summus vir et imperator, Acci, amicissimi sui, carminibus templorum ac monumentorum aditus exornavit suorum. Iam vero ille qui cum Aetolis Ennio comite bellavit Fulvius non dubitavit Martis manubias Musis consecrare.

5 Quare, in qua urbe imperatores prope armati poetarum nomen et Musarum delubra coluerunt, in ea non debent togati iudices a Musarum honore et a poetarum salute abhorrere.

SHORT ANSWER QUESTIONS

1. Why does Cicero bring the generals Decimus Brutus and Fulvius into his argument?

2. How does he use their examples to provoke the jury? What figure of speech does he employ (line 4)? Give the Latin and English.

3. Who is *Ennio comite* (line 3) and in what context was he seen earlier?

OTHER QUESTIONS

1. Give the case and reason for that case for

   (a) *Acci* (line 1). Briefly identify this person.

   (b) *aditus* (line 2)

   (c) *Martis* (line 4)

   (d) *armati* (line 5), *togati* (line 6). What does each modify? How does Cicero highlight the contrast?

ESSAY QUESTION

In sections 19 (below) and 27 (above), Cicero describes the treatment of the poet and literary artist. What universal examples and what specific persons are mentioned and why? Why do you think he included military generals in his argument? Be sure to cite the Latin (with English) that supports your ideas.

19. Sit igitur, iudices, sanctum apud vos, humanissimos homines, hoc poetae nomen quod nulla umquam barbaria violavit. Saxa atque solitudines voci respondent, bestiae saepe immanes cantu flectuntur atque consistunt; nos instituti rebus optimis non poetarum voce moveamur?

5 Homerum Colophonii civem esse dicunt suum, Chii suum vindicant, 5 Salaminii repetunt, Smyrnaei vero suum esse confirmant itaque etiam delubrum eius in oppido dedicaverunt, permulti alii praeterea pugnant inter se atque contendunt. Ergo illi alienum, quia poeta fuit, post mortem etiam expetunt; nos hunc vivum qui et voluntate et legibus noster est

10 repudiamus, praesertim cum omne olim studium atque omne ingenium contulerit Archias ad populi Romani gloriam laudemque celebrandam? Nam et Cimbricas res adulescens attigit et ipsi illi C. Mario qui durior ad haec studia videbatur iucundus fuit.

28. Atque ut id libentius faciatis, iam me vobis, iudices, indicabo
et de meo quodam amore gloriae nimis acri fortasse, verum tamen honesto
vobis confitebor. Nam quas res nos in consulatu nostro vobiscum simul
pro salute huius urbis atque imperi et pro vita civium proque universa re
5   publica gessimus, attigit hic versibus atque inchoavit. Quibus auditis,
quod mihi magna res et iucunda visa est, hunc ad perficiendum adornavi.
Nullam enim virtus aliam mercedem laborum periculorumque desiderat
praeter hanc laudis et gloriae. Qua quidem detracta, iudices, quid est
quod in hoc tam exiguo vitae curriculo et tam brevi tantis nos in laboribus
10   exerceamus?

Short Answer Questions

1. In the passage above, Cicero confesses to the jury one of his great desires. In a short essay, discuss how Cicero defends this desire and Archias' role in the pursuit of it.

2. To what specific event does *res nos in consulatu nostro* (line 3)?

3. What is meant by *magna res* (line 6)?

Other Questions

1. What part of speech is *libentius* (line 1)? Translate it.

2. To whom or what does *hic* refer (line 5)?

3. What construction is *Quibus auditis* (line 5)? What would be a good translation for it?

4. Translate the sentence *Nullam . . . gloriae* (lines 7–8).

29. Certe, si nihil animus praesentiret in posterum, et si, quibus regionibus vitae spatium circumscriptum est, isdem omnis cogitationes terminaret suas, nec tantis se laboribus frangeret neque tot curis vigiliisque angeretur nec totiens de ipsa vita dimicaret. Nunc insidet quaedam in optimo quoque

5   virtus, quae noctes ac dies animum gloriae stimulis concitat atque admonet non cum vitae tempore esse dimittendam commemorationem nominis nostri, sed cum omni posteritate adaequandam.

SHORT ANSWER QUESTIONS

1. According to Cicero, how is the mind responsible for its own feelings about hardship, anxiety, and the struggle for life itself (lines 1–4)?

2. Describe the specific quality Cicero mentions in each noble person that accounts for such activity of the mind (lines 4–7).

3. Cicero uses an abundance of time words in this passage to make his point about glory. Cite some of these time words and briefly discuss their impact on the section.

OTHER QUESTIONS

1. Give the mood, usage, and translation for

   (a) *praesentiret* (line 1)

   (b) *frangeret* (line 3)

2. What figure of speech is seen in lines 3–4 and how does it enhance the meaning of the passage?

30. An vero tam parvi animi videamur esse omnes qui in re publica atque in his vitae periculis laboribusque versamur ut, cum usque ad extremum spatium nullum tranquillum atque otiosum spiritum duxerimus, nobiscum simul moritura omnia arbitremur? An statuas et imagines, non
5   animorum simulacra, sed corporum, studiose multi summi homines reliquerunt; consiliorum relinquere ac virtutum nostrarum effigiem nonne multo malle debemus summis ingeniis expressam et politam? Ego vero omnia quae gerebam iam tum in gerendo spargere me ac disseminare arbitrabar in orbis terrae memoriam sempiternam. Haec vero sive a meo
10   sensu post mortem afutura est, sive, ut sapientissimi homines putaverunt, ad aliquam animi mei partem pertinebit, nunc quidem certe cogitatione quadam speque delector.

Short Answer Questions

1. In this chapter, Cicero poses questions and makes a personal comment about the afterlife. How and why does he wish to alter the custom of *imagines* (lines 4–7)? What hope sustains and delights him as he considers life after death (lines 9–12)?

Other Questions

1. Give the mood, usage, and translation for

   (a) *videamur* (line 1)

   (b) *duxerimus* (line 3)

   (c) *arbitremur* (line 4)

2. Give the case and reason for that case for

   (a) *animi* (line 1)

   (b) *quae* (line 8)

   (c) *haec* (line 9) To what does it refer?

3. What part of speech is *multo* (line 7)? Identify its case and the reason for that case.

ESSAY QUESTION

In sections 14 (below) and 30 (cf. p. 62), Cicero uses the word *imagines* to strengthen his discussion on the value of literature. Identify how he uses the term in each section: what function did they serve and under what conditions? How did Cicero himself make use of them in his own life? Does he seem consistent in each discussion? Use specific Latin from each section to support your statements.

14. Nam nisi multorum praeceptis multisque litteris mihi ab
adulescentia suasissem nihil esse in vita magno opere expetendum nisi
laudem atque honestatem, in ea autem persequenda omnis cruciatus corporis,
omnia pericula mortis atque exsili parvi esse ducenda, numquam me pro
5   salute vestra in tot ac tantas dimicationes atque in hos profligatorum
hominum cotidianos impetus obiecissem. Sed pleni omnes sunt libri, plenae
sapientium voces, plena exemplorum vetustas; quae iacerent in tenebris
omnia, nisi litterarum lumen accederet. Quam multas nobis imagines non
solum ad intuendum verum etiam ad imitandum fortissimorum virorum
10   expressas scriptores et Graeci et Latini reliquerunt! Quas ego mihi
semper in administranda re publica proponens animum et mentem meam
ipsa cogitatione hominum excellentium conformabam.

31. Quare conservate, iudices, hominem pudore eo quem amicorum
videtis comprobari cum dignitate, tum etiam vetustate, ingenio autem tanto
quantum id convenit existimari, quod summorum hominum iudiciis
expetitum esse videatis, causa vero eius modi quae beneficio legis,

5   auctoritate municipi, testimonio Luculli, tabulis Metelli comprobetur.
Quae cum ita sint, petimus a vobis, iudices, si qua non modo humana
verum etiam divina in tantis ingeniis commendatio debet esse, ut eum
qui vos, qui vestros imperatores, qui populi Romani res gestas semper
ornavit, qui etiam his recentibus nostris vestrisque domesticis periculis

10   aeternum se testimonium laudis daturum esse profitetur, quique est ex
eo numero qui semper apud omnis sancti sunt habiti itaque dicti, sic in
vestram accipiatis fidem ut humanitate vestra levatus potius quam
acerbitate violatus esse videatur.

SHORT ANSWER QUESTIONS

1. What is the significance of the word *Quare* (line 1)? For what is the audience being prepared? What is this section of a speech called and what is its purpose?

2. What do the friends of Archias contribute to his honor (lines 1–3)?

3. To what does *municipi* (line 5) refer, both generally and specifically?

4. What proof does Cicero repeat in his summary argument to prove his case (lines 3–5)?

5. Where is the focus of the section placed by the repetition of *qui* five times in lines 7–10?

6. Give Cicero's rationale why the jury should offer Archias its trust (lines 7–13).

OTHER QUESTIONS

1. Give the case and reason for that case for

    (a) *pudore* (line 1)

    (b) *quae* (line 4)

    (c) *qua* (line 6)

    (d) *omnis* (line 11)

2. Translate *sic . . . videatur* (lines 11–13).

32. Quae de causa pro mea consuetudine breviter simpliciterque
dixi, iudices, ea confido probata esse omnibus; quae a foro aliena
iudicialique consuetudine et de hominis ingenio et communiter
de ipso studio locutus sum, ea, iudices, a vobis spero esse in bonam
5   partem accepta, ab eo qui iudicium exercet, certo scio.

SHORT ANSWER QUESTIONS

1. Translate this section as literally as you can into good English.

2. To whom does *qui iudicium exercet* (line 5) refer? What relation is he to Cicero?

OTHER QUESTIONS

1. Give the case and reason for that case for

    (a) *Quae* (line 1)

    (b) *aliena* (line 2)

    (c) *iudicalique* (line 3)

    (d) *ea* (line 4)

    (e) *vobis* (line 4)

    (f) *iudicium* (line 5)

2. What part of speech are *breviter, simpliciter,* and *communiter* (lines 1–3)?

ANSWERS TO SAMPLE ASSESSMENT QUESTIONS

1. Si quid est in me ingeni, iudices, quod sentio quam sit exiguum, aut si
qua exercitatio dicendi, in qua me non infitior mediocriter esse versatum,
aut si huiusce rei ratio aliqua ab optimarum artium studiis ac disciplina
profecta, a qua ego nullum confiteor aetatis meae tempus abhorruisse,
5 earum rerum omnium vel in primis hic A. Licinius fructum a me repetere
prope suo iure debet. Nam quoad longissime potest mens mea respicere
spatium praeteriti temporis et pueritiae memoriam recordari ultimam, inde
usque repetens, hunc video mihi principem et ad suscipiendam et ad
ingrediendam rationem horum studiorum exstitisse. Quod si haec vox
10 huius hortatu praeceptisque conformata non nullis aliquando saluti fuit,
a quo id accepimus quo ceteris opitulari et alios servare possemus, huic
profecto ipsi, quantum est situm in nobis, et opem et salutem ferre debemus.

SHORT ANSWER QUESTIONS

1. Who is A. Licinius (line 5)? Give his complete Latin name.

   Aulus Licinius Archias was a famous professional poet who wrote in Greek. He was born in Antioch, Syria, and traveled throughout the Greek East, to southern Italy, and to Rome.

2. In lines 1–6 (*Si . . . debet*), Cicero states that, under certain conditions, Archias should demand the benefit of all the orator's studies. Describe two of the three conditions Cicero lists.

   The three conditions are if Cicero has any natural ability, or any skill in speaking, or any methodology of this skill which he derived from the study of liberal arts.

3. When Cicero looks back to his childhood, specifically how does he say that Archias stood out?

   Archias was foremost in prompting Cicero to undertake and follow a study of the liberal arts.

4. Find one example each of chiasmus and litotes in this section.

   chiasmus: *nullum aetatis meae tempus* **(line 4);** *spatium praeteriti temporis et pueritiae memoriam* **(line 7) and** *vox hortatu praeceptisque conformata* **(lines 9–10); litotes:** *non nullis* **(line 10)**

5. Name one figure of speech seen in this section and write out the Latin that illustrates it (excluding litotes and chiasmus).

   tricolon crescens (three conditions in sentence one with accompanying three relative clauses); anaphora

6. In lines 9–12 (*Quod . . . debemus*), what specific training did Cicero receive from Archias and how did it influence Cicero's dealings with others?

Archias trained Cicero in oratory. He helped bring aid and safety to others.

OTHER QUESTIONS

1. Give the case and reason for that case for

    (a) *ingeni* (line 1)

    partitive genitive

    (b) *me* (line 2)

    accusative, subject of indirect statement

    (c) *ad suscipiendam et ad ingrediendam rationem* (lines 8–9)

    accusative gerundive in a purpose clause

    (d) *nullis . . . saluti* (line 10)

    double dative (*nullis*, advantage/reference, *saluti*, purpose)

2. What is the use of the subjunctive *sit* (line 1)?

indirect question

3. Write the full Latin form of the word *quid* (line 1).

aliquid

2. Ac ne quis a nobis hoc ita dici forte miretur, quod alia quaedam in hoc facultas sit ingeni neque haec dicendi ratio aut disciplina, ne nos quidem huic uni studio penitus umquam dediti fuimus. Etenim omnes artes quae ad humanitatem pertinent habent quoddam commune vinculum et quasi

5   cognatione quadam inter se continentur.

SHORT ANSWER QUESTIONS

1. What is Cicero's comment about the arts that pertain to civilization?

   They have a common bond and are held together by a certain kinship.

OTHER QUESTIONS

1. Give the mood and syntax for

   (a) *miretur* (line 1)

   subjunctive, purpose clause

   (b) *dici* (line 1)

   infinitive, indirect statement

   (c) *sit* (line 2)

   subjunctive, subordinate clause in indirect statement

2. What tone is expressed by Cicero in line 2 with the phrase *ne nos quidem*?

   proud, self-congratulatory

3. Sed ne cui vestrum mirum esse videatur me in quaestione legitima et in
iudicio publico, cum res agatur apud praetorem populi Romani, lectissimum
virum, et apud severissimos iudices, tanto conventu hominum ac frequentia,
hoc uti genere dicendi, quod non modo a consuetudine iudiciorum verum

5   etiam a forensi sermone abhorreat, quaeso a vobis ut in hac causa mihi
detis hanc veniam accommodatam huic reo, vobis, quemadmodum
spero, non molestam, ut me pro summo poeta atque eruditissimo homine
dicentem hoc concursu hominum litteratissimorum, hac vestra humanitate,
hoc denique praetore exercente iudicium, patiamini de studiis humanitatis

10   ac litterarum paulo loqui liberius, et in eius modi persona quae propter
otium ac studium minime in iudiciis periculisque tractata est uti prope
novo quodam et inusitato genere dicendi.

SHORT ANSWER QUESTIONS

1. In lines 1–5 (*Sed . . . abhorreat*), why might the jury wonder at Cicero's type of speaking in this court case?

   It is a type of speaking not customary for court cases and forensic language.

2. Cicero flatters several individuals and groups here. Give two examples, citing the Latin and English of such comments.

   Cicero flatters the praetor with the phrase *praetorem . . . lectissimum virum* (a most excellent man, line 2), the jurors by saying that they are *severissimos iudices* (very strict jurors, line 3) and the poet with the phrase *summo poeta . . . eruditissimo homine* (a very great poet and very learned man, line 7).

3. What two figures of speech are seen in lines 8–9 (*hoc concursu . . . iudicium*), and how are they representative of Ciceronian style?

   The two figures are anaphora (*hoc, hac, hoc*) and tricolon crescens (the three ablative phrases). Cicero often uses anaphora for emphasis along with tricolon crescens which has a balancing effect.

4. Give an example of hendiadys in this section.

   in iudiciis periculisque

5. How has Archias spent his time instead of risking the hazards of the courtroom (lines 10–11)?

   quiet study

6. Why do you think Cicero has included a number of superlatives in this section? What effect does this create?

   It makes his entire discussion about the new procedure seem very worthwhile. It also flatters those from whom he makes the request.

Other Questions

1. Give the case and reason for that case for

    (a) *vestrum* (line 1)

    partitive genitive

    (b) *genere* (line 4)

    ablative with *uti*

2. Give the mood and usage for

    (a) *videatur* (line 1)

    subjunctive, purpose

    (b) *detis* (line 6)

    subjunctive, indirect command

    (c) *loqui* (line 10)

    infintive, indirect statement

3. What part of speech is *liberius* (line 10)?

    adverb, comparative

Essay Question

To defend Archias successfully, Cicero decided upon a less customary courtroom procedure. In a well-written essay, describe his new approach and include how Cicero approaches the jury, requests the exception he wants, and defends his request. What Ciceronian elements (e.g., rhetorical devices, word placement) are evident and how do they help his case? Be sure to include the Latin (translated or paraphrased into English) that supports your ideas.

Students must mention how Cicero wants to speak more freely on cultural matters. They should include that his approach is respectful, maybe even overdone (superlatives). He asks courteously, *even anticipating their possible reaction (*molestam*), and defends his request by reminding the jury that Archias is a man untrained in the courtroom scene (*minime in iudiciis periculisque tractata est*). Cicero would like an approach suitable for this defendant. His manner is conciliatory and polite (things such as word choice, placement, and figures of speech should be included) to enhance his cause.

---

* Ideas marked with an asterisk are optional, not required items that must be included in a student's essay.

4. Quod si mihi a vobis tribui concedique sentiam, perficiam profecto
ut hunc A. Licinium non modo non segregandum, cum sit civis,
a numero civium verum etiam, si non esset, putetis asciscendum fuisse.

5   Nam, ut primum ex pueris excessit Archias atque ab eis artibus quibus
aetas puerilis ad humanitatem informari solet, se ad scribendi studium
contulit. Primum Antiochiae—nam ibi natus est loco nobili—celebri quondam
urbe et copiosa atque eruditissimis hominibus liberalissimisque studiis
adfluenti, celeriter antecellere omnibus ingeni gloria coepit. Post
in ceteris Asiae partibus cunctaque Graecia sic eius adventus celebrabantur

10   ut famam ingeni exspectatio hominis, exspectationem ipsius adventus
admiratioque superaret.

Short Answer Questions

1. Translate lines 1–3 (*Quod . . . fuisse*).

   "But if I should feel that it is bestowed and is granted to me by you, I would bring it about without question that you think that Aulus Licinius here not only should not have been excluded from the number of citizens, since he is a citizen, but also that, if he were not a citizen, you would think that he ought to have been enrolled."

2. To what did Archias apply himself after boyhood (lines 4–6)? Was he successful?

   Archias applied himself to the pursuit of writing, and he quickly began to surpass everyone.

3. How does Cicero describe the city of Antioch when Archias lived there?

   Cicero describes Antioch as rich, well-populated, filled with very learned men and a liberal culture.

4. In lines 8–11 (*Post . . . superaret*), what does Cicero tell us about the people's reactions to Archias in Asia and Greece?

   People crowded around in great anticipation to see him arrive, and their admiration for him exceeded their anticipation.

5. List examples of and comment on Cicero's use of superlatives in this section.

   The Latin phrase, *eruditissimis hominibus liberalissimisque studiis* (line 7), enhances the picture of Antioch as a place of learning and liberal studies.

6. Lines 1–3 of this section marks the end of what element of a formal oration? In the second part of a formal speech, called the *narratio* (*Nam, ut primum . . .*), what does the speaker do?

   It marks the end of the *exordium*. The speaker summarizes the facts which lead up to the main issue.

OTHER QUESTIONS

1. Give the case and reason for that case for

   (a) *Antiochiae* (line 6)

   locative, place where

   (b) *loco* (line 6)

   ablative, description

   (c) *omnibus* (line 8)

   dative, with *antecellere*

   (d) *gloria* (line 8)

   ablative, respect

   (e) *ipsius* (line 10)

   genitive, objective

5. Erat Italia tum plena Graecarum artium ac disciplinarum, studiaque
haec et in Latio vehementius tum colebantur quam nunc isdem in oppidis,
et hic Romae propter tranquillitatem rei publicae non neglegebantur. Itaque
hunc et Tarentini et Locrenses et Regini et Neapolitani civitate ceterisque

5   praemiis donarunt, et omnes qui aliquid de ingeniis poterant iudicare
cognitione atque hospitio dignum existimarunt. Hac tanta celebritate
famae cum esset iam absentibus notus, Romam venit Mario consule et
Catulo. Nactus est primum consules eos quorum alter res ad scribendum
maximas, alter cum res gestas tum etiam studium atque auris adhibere

10   posset. Statim Luculli, cum praetextatus etiam tum Archias esset, eum
domum suam receperunt. Dedit etiam hoc non solum lumen ingeni ac litterarum,
verum etiam naturae atque virtutis ut domus, quae huius adulescentiae
prima favit, eadem esset familiarissima senectuti.

Short Answer Questions

1. During the time period in this section, how receptive were Latium and Rome itself to Greek arts and studies?

   Latium energetically pursued these studies; Rome, free of the burdens of war, did not neglect them.

2. How did the peoples of southern Italy respond to the abilities of Archias (lines 3–6)?

   They considered him worthy of knowing and received him as a guest.

3. When Archias came to Rome, what did each of the two consuls, Marius and Catulus, offer to his literary talents (lines 8–10)?

   Marius provided very great things (*maximas res*) to write about; Catulus gave him accomplishments and his attention (*studium atque auris*).

4. What part did the house of the Luculli play in the life of Archias (lines 10–13)?

   When Archias was young (still in his *toga praetexta*), the Luculli took him into their home. Even into his old age, Archias remained very close to the family (*domus . . . familiarissima senectuti*, lines 12–13).

OTHER QUESTIONS

1. Give the case and reason for that case for

    (a) *cognitione et hospitio* (line 6)

      ablative with *dignum*

    (b) *Mario consule et Catulo* (lines 7–8)

      ablative, time when (or ablative absolute)

    (c) *adulescentiae* (line 12)

      dative with *favit*

2. Why is *esset* (line 10) in the subjunctive?

    circumstantial clause

ESSAY QUESTION

For Cicero, proving the citizenship of Archias was more than citing documents. Using Latin (with English translation/paraphrase) to support your answer, write an essay describing how, in this section, Cicero emphasizes the connection of the poet to Italy and Rome. How well did he fit in? What factors affected his status in the cultural and social life of the city? Provide specific examples. Include at least one figure of speech in your essay and discuss howit enhances this passage.

Cicero quickly shifts to a discussion of literature and its place in the society of Magna Graecia and Rome. Students should comment on the wealth of Greek culture already in southern Italy by that time and Cicero's confirmation of that in his day. They should note the particular behavior toward Archias of the peoples mentioned and continue by describing his very positive reception when he went to Rome. Again, specifics should be detailed about his treatment by *Catulus or Marius, but especially by the Luculli, since mention is made of the lifelong friendship Archias enjoyed with them.

6. Erat temporibus illis iucundus Q. Metello, illi Numidico, et eius
Pio filio, audiebatur a M. Aemilio, vivebat cum Q. Catulo et patre et
filio, a L. Crasso colebatur. Lucullos vero et Drusum et Octavios et
Catonem et totam Hortensiorum domum devinctam consuetudine cum
5   teneret, adficiebatur summo honore, quod eum non solum colebant,
qui aliquid percipere atque audire studebant, verum etiam si qui forte
simulabant. Interim satis longo intervallo, cum esset cum M. Lucullo
in Siciliam profectus et cum ex ea provincia cum eodem Lucullo
decederet, venit Heracleam. Quae cum esset civitas aequissimo iure
10   ac foedere, ascribi se in eam civitatem voluit idque, cum ipse per se
dignus putaretur, tum auctoritate et gratia Luculli ab Heracliensibus
impetravit.

SHORT ANSWER QUESTIONS

1. In lines 1–7 Cicero mentions Archias' acceptance by several notable Romans. Select three and describe how each showed his approval of the poet.

   Q. Metellus and M. Aemilius were friends who listened to his readings; Q. Catulus and his son offered their home to him; L. Crassus cultivated a friendship with him; the Luculli, Octavii, Drusus, Cato, and and the whole Hortensian household were bound to him by close ties.

2. What relationship did the city of Heraclea have with Rome (lines 9–10)? Why did Archias want to be enrolled as a citizen there?

   It enjoyed the most equal (full) civic rights.

3. How did Archias obtain citizenship in Heraclea (lines 11–12)?

   He obtained citizenship through the influence and prestige of Lucullus.

OTHER QUESTIONS

1. Give the case and reason for that case for

   (a) *Metello* (line 1)

   dative with *iucundus*

   (b) *idque* (line 10)

   accusative, direct object of *impetravit*

2. Identify the subject of *esset* (line 7).

   Archias

7. Data est civitas Silvani lege et Carbonis: Sɪ ǫᴜɪ ꜰᴏᴇᴅᴇʀᴀᴛɪꜱ ᴄɪᴠɪᴛᴀᴛɪʙᴜꜱ ᴀꜱᴄʀɪᴘᴛɪ ꜰᴜɪꜱꜱᴇɴᴛ, ꜱɪ ᴛᴜᴍ ᴄᴜᴍ ʟᴇx ꜰᴇʀᴇʙᴀᴛᴜʀ ɪɴ Iᴛᴀʟɪᴀ ᴅᴏᴍɪᴄɪʟɪᴜᴍ ʜᴀʙᴜɪꜱꜱᴇɴᴛ ᴇᴛ ꜱɪ ꜱᴇxᴀɢɪɴᴛᴀ ᴅɪᴇʙᴜꜱ ᴀᴘᴜᴅ ᴘʀᴀᴇᴛᴏʀᴇᴍ ᴇꜱꜱᴇɴᴛ ᴘʀᴏꜰᴇꜱꜱɪ. Cum hic domicilium Romae multos iam annos haberet, professus est apud praetorem Q. Metel-
5   lum, familiarissimum suum.

Short Answer Questions

1. According to the law of Silvanus and Carbo, what two conditions had to be met for citizenship in states allied to Rome (lines 1–3)?

   To have a residence in Italy when the law was enacted and to have professed citizenship within 60 days to the praetor were the two conditions.

2. Briefly explain how Archias fulfilled these requirements (lines 3–5).

   He had had a home in Rome for many years and had reported to the praetor.

Other Questions

1. What tense and mood are the verbs *fuissent* and *habuissent* (line 2)?

   pluperfect subjunctive

2. What is the case and reason for that case for *diebus* (line 3)?

   ablative, time when

3. What is the best translation for *Cum* (line 3)?

   since

4. To whom does *suum* (line 5) refer?

   Archias

8. Si nihil aliud nisi de civitate ac lege dicimus, nihil dico amplius: causa dicta est. Quid enim horum informari, Gratti, potest? Heracleaene esse tum ascriptum negabis? Adest vir summa auctoritate et religione et fide, M. Lucullus, qui se non opinari

5　　sed scire, non audisse sed vidisse, non interfuisse sed egisse dicit. Adsunt Heraclienses legati, nobilissimi homines, huius iudici causa cum mandatis et cum publico testimonio venerunt, qui hunc ascriptum Heracleae esse dicunt. Hic tu tabulas desideras Hercliensium publicas, quas Italico bello incenso tabulario interisse scimus omnes? Est

10　　ridiculum ad ea quae habemus nihil dicere, quaerere quae habere non possumus, et de hominum memoria tacere, litterarum memoriam flagitare et, cum habeas amplissimi viri religionem, integerrimi municipi ius iurandum fidemque, ea quae depravari nullo modo possunt repudiare, tabulas quas idem dicis solere corrumpi desiderare.

Short Answer Questions

1. According to Cicero, how did M. Lucullus help prove the citizenship of Archias (lines 3–5)?

   Lucullus had high prestige, loyalty, and religious devotion. In addition, Metellus says that he knows (the citizenship) is true: he did not hear about it but saw it and was not merely present but brought it about.

2. What weight did the Heraclean envoys provide (lines 6–8)? How useful were the public records of Heraclea (lines 8–9)?

   They were all most noble; they were destroyed in a fire.

3. At the end of this section, Cicero criticizes Grattius' demand for more proof as *ridiculum*. Give three examples from Cicero's list of his opponent's demands.

   He says nothing about the things available; he requests unattainable things; he is silent about men's memory of the events; he insists on written evidence.

4. Section 8 begins the third part of a classical speech. What is this element called and what is its purpose?

   The third part, called the *refutatio*, is a counter-argument to the prosecution.

OTHER QUESTIONS

1. Give the case and reason for that case for for

    (a) *Gratti* (line 2)

    vocative, direct address

    (b) *Heracleae* (line 3)

    locative, place where

    (c) *auctoritate et religione et fide* (line 4)

    ablative, description

    (d) *se* (line 4)

    accusative, subject of indirect statement

    (e) *huius iudici* (line 6)

    genitive with *causa*

    (f) *quas* (line 9)

    accusative, subject of indirect statement

    (g) *quae* (line 10)

    accusative, direct object (*habere non possumus*)

2. Give the mood and usage for

    (a) *opinari* (line 4)

    infinitive, indirect statement

    (b) *habeas* (line 12)

    subjunctive, circumstantial clause

9. An domicilium Romae non habuit is qui tot annis ante civitatem
datam sedem omnium rerum ac fortunarum suarum Romae conlocavit?
An non est professus? Immo vero eis tabulis professus quae solae
ex illa professione conlegioque praetorum obtinent publicarum
5   tabularum auctoritatem. Nam, cum Appi tabulae neglegentius
adservatae dicerentur, Gabini, quam diu incolumis fuit, levitas,
post damnationem calamitas omnem tabularum fidem resignasset,
Metellus, homo sanctissimus modestissimusque omnium, tanta
diligentia fuit ut ad L. Lentulum praetorem et ad iudices venerit
10   et unius nominis litura se commotum esse dixerit. His igitur in
tabulis nullam lituram in nomine A. Licini videtis.

Short Answer Questions

1. Comment on the reliability of the public records mentioned above:

    (a)   in which Archias was registered (lines 3–5)

    They are the only documents which have the authority of public records.

    (b)   of Appius (lines 5–6)

    They were kept rather carelessly.

    (c)   of Gabinius (lines 6–7)

    Their authenticity was weakened by Gabinius' frivolous behavior before his conviction and by the resulting disaster after his conviction.

2. How did Metellus show exemplary behavior (lines 8–10)?

    He went to the praetor and panel of judges to express his concern about the erasure of one name.

Other Questions

1. Give the case and reason for that case for

    (a)   *Romae* (line 1)

    locative, place where

    (b)   *levitas* (line 6)

    nominative, subject

    (c)   *se* (line 10)

    accusative, subject of indirect statement

2. What is the tense of *resignasset* (line 7)? Write the full Latin form of this verb.

    pluperfect subjunctive, *resignavisset*.

10. Quae cum ita sint, quid est quod de eius civitate dubitetis,
praesertim cum aliis quoque in civitatibus fuerit ascriptus? Etenim
cum mediocribus multis et aut nulla aut humili aliqua arte praeditis
gratuito civitatem in Graecia homines impertiebant, Reginos credo

5   aut Locrensis aut Neapolitanos aut Tarentinos, quod scaenicis
artificibus largiri solebant, id huic summa ingeni praedito gloria
noluisse! Quid? Cum ceteri non modo post civitatem datam sed
etiam post legem Papiam aliquo modo in eorum municipiorum tabulas
inrepserunt, hic qui ne utitur quidem illis in quibus est scriptus, quod

10 semper se Heracliensem esse voluit, reicietur?

SHORT ANSWER QUESTIONS

1. Comment on how Cicero contrasts the situation of Archias concerning citizenship when compared to

    (a) persons in Magna Graecia (lines 2–4)

    Citizenship was freely granted to people with mediocre abilities and those with little or no talent (as contrasted with the great skill of Archias).

    (b) actors (lines 4–6)

    The people of Rhegium, Neapolis, and Tarentum customarily bestowed citizenship on actors (Archias was endowed with great talent).

    (c) others after the *Lex Papia* was passed (lines 7–10)

    They somehow crept into the public records, gaining citizenship (Archias was already enrolled in certain records, wants Heraclean status).

2. Where do we see Cicero's use of irony in this passage? Cite the Latin used and briefly explain its application here.

    credo **(line 4), "well, I suppose . . . "; "am I to believe . . .?"** *Quid?* **(line 7), "well, what about . . ." The first comment expresses an opposite feeling (he actually does not believe this at all); the other comment is a rhetorical question, again with a note of disbelief (e.g., "look at this!, can you believe this?")**

OTHER QUESTIONS

1. What is the best translation for *cum* (line 1)?

    since

2. To whom or what does *huic* (line 6) refer?

    Archias

3. What is the tense of the verb *reicietur* (line 10)?

    future tense

11. Census nostros requiris. Scilicet! Est enim obscurum proximis
censoribus hunc cum clarissimo imperatore L. Lucullo apud exercitum
fuisse, superioribus cum eodem quaestore fuisse in Asia, primis Iulio
et Crasso nullam populi partem esse censam. Sed, quoniam census
5   non ius civitatis confirmat ac tantum modo indicat eum, qui sit census,
ita se iam tum gessisse pro cive, eis temporibus is quem tu criminaris
ne ipsius quidem iudicio in civium Romanorum iure esse versatum et
testamentum saepe fecit nostris legibus, et adiit hereditates civium
Romanorum, et in beneficiis ad aerarium delatus est a L. Lucullo
10   pro consule. Quaere argumenta, si quae potes; numquam enim hic
neque suo neque amicorum iudicio revincetur.

Short Answer Questions

1. How does Cicero explain why Archias has not been on the last three census lists of citizens (lines 1–3)?

    Regarding the most recent lists, Archias was with the general Lucullus and his army; before that, he was with Lucullus again (as praetor) in Asia; in the first set, when Iulius and Crassus were censors, no part of the citizenry was enrolled.

2. Using the information Cicero gives,

    (a) what do census lists show regarding citizenship (lines 4–6)?

    A person whose name was put on the citizen list had acted like a citizen (does not prove citizenship).

    (b) specifically how does Archias, therefore, qualify for citizenship (lines 7–10)?

    He often made his will in accordance with Roman law, shared in inheritances of Roman citizens, and was named by Lucullus to the treasury (for a monetary award).

3. What tone is expressed by Cicero through his use of *Scilicet* (line 1), and how does he continue this tone in the next sentence?

    The ironic tone is expressed by saying it is not clear (*Est enim obscurum*, line 1) that he was with Lucullus and his army (while implying the question, "how could it not be clear?").

OTHER QUESTIONS

1. Give the mood and usage for

    (a) *fuisse* (line 3)

      infinitive in indirect statement

    (b) *sit* (line 5)

      subjunctive, relative clause of characteristic

    (c) *criminaris* (line 6)

      indicative, stating a fact

    (d) *Quaere* (line 10)

      imperative, command

2. To whom does *is* (line 6) refer?

   Archias

12. Quaeres a nobis, Gratti, cur tanto opere hoc homine delectemur.
Quia suppeditat nobis ubi et animus ex hoc forensi strepitu reficiatur
et aures convicio defessae conquiescant. An tu existimas aut suppetere
nobis posse quod cotidie dicamus in tanta varietate rerum, nisi animos
5   nostros doctrina excolamus, aut ferre animos tantam posse contentionem,
nisi eos doctrina eadem relaxemus? Ego vero fateor me his studiis esse
deditum. Ceteros pudeat, si qui ita se litteris abdiderunt ut nihil possint
ex eis neque ad communem adferre fructum neque in aspectum lucemque
proferre; me autem quid pudeat qui tot annos ita vivo, iudices, ut a nullius
10   umquam me tempore aut commodo aut otium meum abstraxerit aut
voluptas avocarit aut denique somnus retardarit?

Short Answer Questions

1. Translate as literally as you can into good English lines 1–6 (*Quaeres . . . relaxemus?*).

   "You will ask from me, Grattius, why I am so greatly charmed by this man. Because he furnishes us (with a place) where both the mind may be refreshed from this noise of the court, and the ears, weary from the clamor, might rest. Or do you think that that which we say everyday on such a variety of things can be available to us if we do not cultivate our minds with formal teaching?"

2. In lines 6–11 (*Ego . . . retardarit*), Cicero criticizes certain kinds of scholars. In a short essay, describe what they do wrong and why he is able to exclude himself from this group.

   They hide themselves in literature, thereby not bringing anything to the common benefit nor to the light. His leisure activities have never prevented him, his pleasures have not called him away, nor has sleep held him back from responding to the needs or interest of anyone.

3. What figure of speech is seen in the phrase *in aspectum lucemque* (line 8)?

   hendiadys

4. The fourth part of an ancient speech begins with this section. What is this part of an oration called and what is its function?

   The fourth part is called the *confirmatio*, an affirmative argument in which the speaker presents his points. Cicero departs from this usual function and discusses the value of liberal arts study to a civilized society.

Other Questions

1. Give the literal and conversational meaning of *tanto opere* (line 1).

   "with such great effort, work" (so greatly)

2. Give the mood and usage for

   (a) *pudeat* (line 7)

   subjunctive, hortatory

   (b) *possint* (line 7)

   subjunctive, result

   (c) *adferre* (line 8)

   infinitive, complementary

3. What is the tense of the verbs *avocarit* and *retardarit* (line 11)? Write their full Latin forms.

   perfect, *avocaverit, retardaverit*

13. Quare quis tandem me reprehendat, aut quis mihi iure suscenseat,
si, quantum ceteris ad suas res obeundas, quantum ad festos dies ludorum
celebrandos, quantum ad alias voluptates et ad ipsam requiem animi et
corporis conceditur temporum, quantum alii tribuunt tempestivis
5   conviviis, quantum denique alveolo, quantum pilae, tantum mihi egomet
ad haec studia recolenda sumpsero? Atque id eo mihi concedendum est
magis quod ex his studiis haec quoque crescit oratio et facultas quae,
quantacumque est in me, numquam amicorum periculis defuit. Quae
si cui levior videtur, illa quidem certe quae summa sunt ex quo fonte
10   hauriam sentio.

SHORT ANSWER QUESTIONS

1. What distinctions does Cicero draw between his activities and those of others in Roman society
   (lines 1–6)?

   **He spends as much time nurturing the study of liberal arts as others spend dealing with their
   personal affairs, celebrating festivals, yielding to other pleasures, resting the body and mind,
   banqueting, playing dice (gambling) or ball.**

2. What talent has Cicero developed as a result of his activities and how has it benefited his friends
   (lines 6–8)?

   Cicero has developed his ability in oratory, and it helps his friends in times of danger.

3. Identify the anaphora in lines 1–6 and discuss briefly the effect it has on the overall point Cicero
   is trying to make in this section.

   Quantum **emphasizes how so much effort is spent on other things rather than on the liberal
   arts.**

4. What figure of speech is seen in the phrase *oratio et facultas* (line 7)?

   hendiadys

5. What specific words used by Cicero create a somewhat self-congratulatory tone in this passage?

   Quantacumque **(line 8),** *quidem certe . . . sentio* **(lines 9–10).**

OTHER QUESTIONS

1. Give the mood and usage for *reprehendat* (line 1).

   subjunctive, potential

2. Write the Latin and English for a gerundive of purpose found in this section.

   ad suas res obeundas **(line 2), for the purpose of carrying out their own affairs;** *ad festos dies ludorum celebrandos* **(lines 2–3), for attending in large crowds the festival days for games;** *ad haec studia recolenda* **(line 6), for the purpose of resuming these studies**

3. Give the case and reason for that case for

   (a) *animi* (line 3)

   genitive, objective

   (b) *mihi* (line 6)

   dative, agent

   (c) *periculis* (line 8)

   ablative with *defuit*

   (d) *Quae* (line 8)

   nominative, subject of *videtur,* **referring to** *oratio*

14. Nam nisi multorum praeceptis multisque litteris mihi ab
adulescentia suasissem nihil esse in vita magno opere expetendum nisi
laudem atque honestatem, in ea autem persequenda omnis cruciatus corporis,
omnia pericula mortis atque exsili parvi esse ducenda, numquam me pro
5   salute vestra in tot ac tantas dimicationes atque in hos profligatorum
hominum cotidianos impetus obiecissem. Sed pleni omnes sunt libri, plenae
sapientium voces, plena exemplorum vetustas; quae iacerent in tenebris
omnia, nisi litterarum lumen accederet. Quam multas nobis imagines non
solum ad intuendum verum etiam ad imitandum fortissimorum virorum
10   expressas scriptores et Graeci et Latini reliquerunt! Quas ego mihi
semper in administranda re publica proponens animum et mentem meam
ipsa cogitatione hominum excellentium conformabam.

Short Answer Questions

1. In lines 1–3, what does Cicero say he has learned from studying literature that are the highest goals in life?

   praise and integrity

2. To what specific historical event does Cicero refer in lines 4–6 (*numquam . . . obiecissem*)?

   the Catilinarian Conspiracy

3. Identify the figure of speech in lines 6–7 and tell how it adds to the impact of the passage.

   anaphora: *pleni, plenae, plena.* **The very word means "full"; its repetition underscores its meaning and the richness of available resources for following the good practices which literature illuminates.**

4. What or who provide guidance in conducting one's life? How? How has Cicero specifically used these resources?

   The many portrait masks of ancestors (in homes) and examples in Greek and Latin authors (of very courageous men) provide guidance. When governing the state, he always kept these examples at the forefront and trained himself by thinking about their outstanding behaviors.

OTHER QUESTIONS

1. Give the mood and usage for

   (a) *suasissem* (line 2)

      subjunctive, past contrary to fact condition

2. What is the case and reason for that case for

   (b) *omnis* (line 3)

      nominative, modifies *cruciatus*

   (c) *sapientium* (line 7)

      genitive, possession

3. What does *proponens* (line 11) modify?

   subject, *ego*

15. Quaeret quispiam: "Quid? Illi ipsi summi viri, quorum virtutes
litteris proditae sunt, istane doctrina quam tu effers laudibus eruditi
fuerunt?" Difficile est hoc de omnibus confirmare, sed tamen est certum
quid respondeam. Ego multos homines excellenti animo ac virtute
5   fuisse et sine doctrina, naturae ipsius habitu prope divino per se ipsos
et moderatos et gravis exstitisse fateor; etiam illud adiungo: saepius
ad laudem atque virtutem naturam sine doctrina quam sine natura
valuisse doctrinam. Atque idem ego hoc contendo: cum ad naturam
eximiam et inlustrem accesserit ratio quaedam conformatioque doctrinae,
10   tum illud nescioquid praeclarum ac singulare solere exsistere.

SHORT ANSWER QUESTIONS

1. In lines 4–6 (*Ego . . . fateor*), what does Cicero admit about those who have not received the type of learning he praises? What figure of speech does he use (line 4)?

   They have had outstanding courage and even have stood out as moderate and serious, with an almost divine quality of talent itself.

2. What are Cicero's comments about character and learning (lines 6–8)?

   Natural talent has had the power to achieve praise and glory without learning more often than learning has had the power to do so without natural talent. Hendiadys (*animo ac virtute*)

3. What occurs when training and natural brilliance are joined (lines 8–10)?

   Something unique and outstanding often comes into being.

OTHER QUESTIONS

1. What is the mood and usage for

   (a) *respondeam* (line 4)

   subjunctive, indirect question

   (b) *exstitisse* (line 6)

   infinitive in indirect statement

   (c) *accesserit* (line 9)

   subjunctive, circumstantial clause

2. What is the case and reason for that case for

   (a) *excellenti animo ac virtute* (line 4)

   ablative, description

   (b) *illud* (line 6)

   accusative, direct object

3. What is the translation of *quam* (line 7)?

   "than"

16. Ex hoc esse hunc numero quem patres nostri viderunt, divinum hominem, Africanum, ex hoc C. Laelium, L. Furium, moderatissimos homines et continentissimos, ex hoc fortissimum virum et illis temporibus doctissimum, M. Catonem illum senem. Qui profecto si nihil ad
5   percipiendam colendamque virtutem litteris adiuvarentur, numquam se ad earum studium contulissent. Quod si non hic tantus fructus ostenderetur, et si ex his studiis delectatio sola peteretur, tamen, ut opinor, hanc animi remissionem humanissimam ac liberalissimam iudicaretis. Nam ceterae neque temporum sunt neque aetatum omnium
10   neque locorum; at haec studia adulescentiam acuunt, senectutem oblectant, secundas res ornant, adversis perfugium ac solacium praebent, delectant domi, non impediunt foris, pernoctant nobiscum, peregrinantur, rusticantur.

SHORT ANSWER QUESTIONS

1. According to Cicero, why did notable Romans like Scipio Africanus and Marcus Cato the Elder pursue the study of literature (lines 4–6)?

   The study of literature helps one attain and cultivate moral integrity and character.

2. How do literary studies surpass other forms of relaxation and enjoyment? Give three examples, citing the Latin and English (lines 9–13).

   They sharpen youth and delight us in old age (*adulescentiam acuunt, senectutem oblectant*); they adorn favorable times (*secundas res adornant*), they provide comfort and refuge in times of crises (*adversis perfugium ac solacium praebent*), they please us at home and do not burden us when outdoors (*delectant domi, non impediunt foris*), and they spend the night with us, travel, and go to the country (*pernoctant nobiscum, peregrinantur, rusticantur*).

3. What is the effect of Cicero's use of superlatives in this section? Use the Latin and English in your discussion.

   Examples of superlatives include *moderatissimos*, "very moderate" (line 2); *continentissimos*, "very restrained" and *fortissimum*, "very brave" (line 3); *doctissimum* "very learned" (line 4); *humanissimam*, "very civilized" and *liberalissimam*, "very gentlemanly" (line 8). The superlatives emphasize the excellence of these men from Roman history and their qualities (at the highest level). He continues to emphasize the powerful connection the study of literature has with the best kind of character.

OTHER QUESTIONS

1. Give the mood and usage for *adiuvarentur* (line 5).

   subjunctive, present contrary to fact conditional

2. Give the case and reason for that case for

   (a) *adversis* (line 11)

      ablative, time when (or attendant circumstance)

   (b) *domi* (line 12)

      locative, place where

3. Keeping the same case, give the comparative of the adjective *fortissimum* (line 3).

   fortiorem

17. Quod si ipsi haec neque attingere neque sensu nostro gustare
possemus, tamen ea mirari deberemus, etiam cum in aliis videremus.
Quis nostrum tam animo agresti ac duro fuit ut Rosci morte nuper
non commoveretur? qui cum esset senex mortuus, tamen propter
5   excellentem artem ac venustatem videbatur omnino mori non
debuisse. Ergo ille corporis motu tantum amorem sibi conciliarat
a nobis omnibus; nos animorum incredibilis motus celeritatemque
ingeniorum neglegemus?

SHORT ANSWER QUESTIONS

1. How does Cicero use the career of Roscius to strengthen his argument for the talents of Archias (lines 4–7)?

   He impressed Cicero and others by the movement of his body. The jury should not neglect the "movement" and special talents of the mind (referring to Archias).

2. Identify and give the Latin for the figure of speech in lines 6–8 (*Ergo . . . neglegemus*).

   chiasmus: *animorum incredibilis motus celeritatemque ingeniorum*

OTHER QUESTIONS

1. Give the tense, mood, and usage for

   (a) *possemus* (line 2)

      imperfect subjunctive, present contrary to fact conditional

   (b) *mori* (line 5)

      present infinitive, complementary

2. Give the case and reason for that case for

   (a) *nostrum* (line 3)

      genitive, partitive

   (b) *animo agresti ac duro* (line 3)

      ablative, description

   (c) *incredibilis* (line 7)

      accusative, modifies *motus*

18. Quotiens ego hunc Archiam vidi, iudices—utar enim vestra
benignitate, quoniam me in hoc novo genere dicendi tam diligenter
attenditis—quotiens ego hunc vidi, cum litteram scripsisset nullam,
magnum numerum optimorum versuum de eis ipsis rebus quae tum
5   agerentur dicere ex tempore, quotiens revocatum eandem rem dicere
commutatis verbis atque sententiis! Quae vero accurate cogitateque
scripsisset, ea sic vidi probari ut ad veterum scriptorum laudem perveniret.
Hunc ego non diligam, non admirer, non omni ratione defendendum putem?
Atque sic a summis hominibus eruditissimisque accepimus, ceterarum
10 rerum studia ex doctrina et praeceptis et arte constare, poetam natura
ipsa valere et mentis viribus excitari et quasi divino quodam spiritu inflari.
Quare suo iure noster ille Ennius "sanctos" appellat poetas, quod quasi
deorum aliquo dono atque munere commendati nobis esse videantur.

SHORT ANSWER QUESTIONS

1. In lines 1–6 (*Quotiens . . . sententiis*) of this section, what specific talent of Archias does Cicero praise? Give the Latin and English.

   Without writing anything down, he spoke a great quantity of the finest verses, and, when asked to do so again, he complied, using brand new expressions (*cum litteram . . . sententiis*).

2. How does Cicero describe the writings of Archias (line 6)? How successful were these writings?

   He wrote carefully and thoughtfully. He earned the praise of old authors.

3. Find an example of a tricolon crescens in this section and provide the Latin.

   non diligam, non admirer, non putem **(line 8)**

4. How have the most learned men distinguished the art of writing poetry from other studies? Who was Ennius and why did he call poets *sanctos* (line 12)?

   An almost divine breath is breathed into them. Ennius was one of the earliest Latin authors (second century, BCE), who wrote the *Annales*, an epic poem. He thought poets were sacred because they seem to be entrusted to us as a gift of the gods.

Other Questions

1. What is the tense, mood, voice, and translation of *utar* (line 1)?

   future, indicative, passive, "I will use"

2. What is the form of *dicendi* (line 2)?

   gerund, genitive

3. To what or whom does *hunc* (line 3) refer?

   Archias

4. What is the case of *revocatum* (line 5) and what does it modify?

   accusative modifying *hunc* (line 3), referring to Archias

5. What part of speech are the words *accurate cogitateque* (line 6)?

   adverbs

6. Why are *diligam, non admirer, non . . . putem* (line 8) in the subjunctive? Translate each one.

   They are deliberative questions. "Should I not cherish, admire, and think . . . "

7. Give the mood and usage of *constare, valere, excitari, inflari* (lines 10–11).

   infinitives in indirect statement, introduced by *accepimus* (line 8), "we have learned"

Essay Question

In defending Archias, Cicero also extolled the study of the liberal arts. In a well-written essay, show how in this section Cicero builds his argument from the specific to the general in his defense of poetry and literature. What rhetorical devices do you think helped his presentation? Why do you think he ended this section in this way?

Students should see the specific application of Archias extemporizing twice, with different verses. The jury was made to see the poet "in action" (anaphora: *quotiens*) with consistency of excellence. The best and the brightest, too, confirm the validity of studying the liberal arts and how poets have something of the divine in them. The ending anchors Cicero's ideas with affirmation from the divine and from tradition. Citing Ennius and his appellation about poets, Cicero grants Archias' position greater strength (poets are a divine gift according to an early, well-respected Latin poet). He moves from the earthly (Archias) to the afterlife (Ennius) and the divine (the gods). Anaphora and tricolon (*non . . . non . . . non*) might be noted.

19. Sit igitur, iudices, sanctum apud vos, humanissimos homines,
hoc poetae nomen quod nulla umquam barbaria violavit. Saxa atque
solitudines voci respondent, bestiae saepe immanes cantu flectuntur
atque consistunt; nos instituti rebus optimis non poetarum voce moveamur?
5   Homerum Colophonii civem esse dicunt suum, Chii suum vindicant,
Salaminii repetunt, Smyrnaei vero suum esse confirmant itaque etiam
delubrum eius in oppido dedicaverunt, permulti alii praeterea pugnant
inter se atque contendunt. Ergo illi alienum, quia poeta fuit, post mortem
etiam expetunt; nos hunc vivum qui et voluntate et legibus noster est
10   repudiamus, praesertim cum omne olim studium atque omne ingenium
contulerit Archias ad populi Romani gloriam laudemque celebrandam?
Nam et Cimbricas res adulescens attigit et ipsi illi C. Mario qui durior
ad haec studia videbatur iucundus fuit.

Short Answer Questions

1. In this section, Cicero exalts the poet in society. In what ways have both men and nature responded to the art of the poet (lines 2–4)?

   No barbarian people have defiled it; rocks, deserted regions, even huge beasts all respond to the poetic voice.

2. Why are the peoples of Colophon, Chios, Salamis, and Smyrna mentioned here (lines 5–7)?

   Each claims Homer as its own citizen.

3. Why does Cicero nearly scold the jury for its possible mistreatment of Archias (lines 8–10)?

   Compared to Homer, who after his death was sought after, even though he was an outsider, they reject a living poet who, by his own will and the laws, is their own.

4. What has Archias done for the Roman people (lines 10–12)? What is the role of Marius in this discussion (lines 12–13)?

   He has brought all his zeal and talent to celebrate the praise and glory of the Roman people. Marius, although seeming to be rather insensitive to such studies, was actually favorable to them.

Other Questions

1. Give the use for the subjunctive and translate each.

    (a) *Sit* (line 1)

         hortatory

    (b) *moveamur* (line 4)

         deliberative question

    (c) *repudiamus* (line 10)

         deliberative question

2. Give the case and reason for that case for

    (a) *saxa* (line 2)

         nominative, subject

    (b) *voci* (line 3)

         dative, indirect object

    (c) *civem* (line 5)

         accusative subject of indirect statement

3. Translate *suum* (line 5). To whom or what does it refer?

    "their own," Colophoni, Chii

4. Translate *hunc* (line 9). To whom or what does it refer?

    "this man," the poet Archias

20. Neque enim quisquam est tam aversus a Musis qui non mandari versibus aeternum suorum laborum praeconium facile patiatur. Themistoclem illum, summum Athenis virum, dixisse aiunt, cum ex eo quaereretur quod acroama aut cuius vocem libentissime audiret: eius

5   a quo sua virtus optime praedicaretur. Itaque ille Marius item eximie L. Plotium dilexit, cuius ingenio putabat ea quae gesserat posse celebrari.

Short Answer Questions

1. What comparison does Cicero make between the Athenian Themistocles and the Roman Marius, although they are separated by nearly four hundred years of history? Give the Latin and English.

   They both wanted their deeds made public through oratory (*a quo sua virtus optime praedicaretur,* **(line 5);** *Plotium dilexit, cuius ingenio putabat ea quae gesserat posse celebrari*).

2. Translate the phrase *aversus a Musis* (line 1) and discuss briefly how it relates to Cicero's purpose here.

   "turned away from the Muses" Even politicians and generals (who might seem far removed from the world of literature) like to have their names and accomplishments celebrated in verse (inspired by the Muses) and made known publicly

3. Identify *L. Plotium* (line 6).

   Lucius Gallus Plotius, a poet, was one of Rome's earliest teachers of formal rhetoric

Other Questions

1. What is the use for each subjunctive?

   (a) *patiatur* (line 2)

   relative clause of characteristic

   (b) *quaereretur* (line 4)

   circumstantial clause

   (c) *praedicaretur* (line 5)

   relative clause of characteristic

2. Give the gender, number, case, and reason for that case of *ea* (line 6).

   neuter, plural, accusative, subject, indirect statement

3. Give the usage of these infinitives.

   (a) *dixisse* (line 3)

   infinitive in indirect statement

   (b) *posse* (line 6)

   infinitive in indirect statement

   (c) *celebrari* (line 7)

   complementary infinitive

21. Mithridaticum vero bellum magnum atque difficile et in multa varietate
terra marique versatum totum ab hoc expressum est; qui libri non modo L.
Lucullum, fortissimum et clarissimum virum, verum etiam populi Romani
nomen inlustrant. Populus enim Romanus aperuit Lucullo imperante Pontum
5   et regiis quondam opibus et ipsa natura et regione vallatum,
    populi Romani exercitus eodem duce non maxima manu innumerabilis
    Armeniorum copias fudit, populi Romani laus est urbem amicissimam
    Cyzicenorum eiusdem consilio ex omni impetu regio atque totius belli ore
    ac faucibus ereptam esse atque servatam. Nostra semper feretur et praedicabitur
10   L. Lucullo dimicante, cum interfectis ducibus depressa hostium classis est,
    incredibilis apud Tenedum pugna illa navalis, nostra sunt tropaea, nostra
    monumenta, nostri triumphi. Quae quorum ingeniis efferuntur, ab eis populi
    Romani fama celebratur.

Short Answer Questions

1. Why was the Mithridatic war difficult (lines 1–2)?

   It took place on land and on sea with much change of fortune.

2. How did Archias glorify the Roman people in his writings about the achievements of Lucius Lucullus (lines 11–13)?

   By giving them most of the credit for the victory under Lucullus' leadership and noting their success against Pontus despite its defensive fortifications, Archias glorified the Roman people.

3. What Latin words represent an example of hendiadys in line 5?

   natura et regione

4. In addition to polyptoton, what figure of speech is seen in the words *Nostra . . . nostra . . . nostra . . . nostri* (lines 10–13)? How does it enhance Cicero's message in this section?

   The anaphora repeats the notion that it was the Roman people who were responsible for victory; their success brought glory, monuments, and triumphs.

Other Questions

1. To whom or what does *hoc* (line 2) refer?

   Archias

2. Give the case and reason for that case for

   (a) *Lucullo imperante* (line 4)

   ablative absolute

   (b) *ipsa natura et regione* (line 5)

   ablative, means

   (c) *interfectis ducibus* (line 10)

   ablative absolute

22. Carus fuit Africano superiori noster Ennius, itaque etiam in
sepulcro Scipionum putatur is esse constitutus ex marmore. At eis
laudibus certe non solum ipse qui laudatur sed etiam populi Romani
nomen ornatur. In caelum huius proavus Cato tollitur; magnus honos
5   populi Romani rebus adiungitur. Omnes denique illi Maximi, Marcelli,
Fulvii non sine communi omnium nostrum laude decorantur. Ergo illum
qui haec fecerat, Rudinum hominem, maiores nostri in civitatem receperunt;
nos hunc Heracliensem, multis civitatibus expetitum, in hac autem legibus
constitutum, de nostra civitate eiciamus?

SHORT ANSWER QUESTIONS

1. At the opening of this section, Cicero comments on the writings of Ennius.

    (a) How was Ennius treated by Scipio the Elder (lines 1–2)?

    Ennius was dear to Scipio, and his statue was placed on the family tomb.

    (b) How did the poetry of Ennius go beyond the mere recording of events (lines 2–5)?

    It cited individuals by name, and the Roman people as a whole were praised equally.

2. Who is *Rudinum hominem* (line 7)? *hunc Heracliensem* (line 8)? How did their treatment by the Roman state differ?

    Ennius (*Rudinum hominem*) was accepted into citizenship. The citizenhip of Archias (*hunc Heracliensem*) is being questioned legally, and he is about to be rejected.

OTHER QUESTIONS

1. Give the case and reason for that case for

    (a) *superiori* (line 1)

    dative, modifies *Africano*

    (b) *Scipionum* (line 2)

    genitive, possession

    (c) *communi* (line 6)

    ablative, modifies *laude*

    (d) *haec* (line 7)

    accusative (neuter plural), substantive acting as direct object

2. To whom or what does *huius* (line 4) refer?

    Cato the Younger, present in the courtroom

3. Translate the verb *eiciamus* (line 9).

    "would we/are we to throw out?"

23. Nam si quis minorem gloriae fructum putat ex Graecis versibus percipi quam ex Latinis, vehementer errat, propterea quod Graeca leguntur in omnibus fere gentibus, Latina suis finibus exiguis sane continentur. Quare, si res eae quas gessimus orbis terrae regionibus definiuntur, cupere debemus,

5   quo hominum nostrorum tela pervenerint, eodem gloriam famamque penetrare, quod cum ipsis populis de quorum rebus scribitur haec ampla sunt, tum eis certe qui de vita gloriae causa dimicant hoc maximum et periculorum incitamentum est et laborum.

SHORT ANSWER QUESTIONS

1. What is the unexpressed noun which *Graeca* (line 2) and *Latina* (line 3) modify?

   verba/scripta.

2. Why does Cicero see no problem if Roman achievements are glorified by a poet writing in Greek rather than Latin (lines 2–3)?

   Cicero says that Greek is read by nearly all peoples; Latin is confined to its narrow boundaries.

3. What other purpose might such writings have besides glorifying deeds of nations (lines 4–8)?

   They might stimulate readers to endure dangers and trials.

OTHER QUESTIONS

1. What is the full form of *quis* (line 1)? Translate the first three words of this sentence.

   aliquis. **"For if anyone . . ."**

2. Give the mood and usage and translate *percipi* (line 1).

   It is an infinitive in indirect statement and translates "is acquired."

3. Give the meaning of *quo* (line 5) and *eodem* (line 5).

   "by which" and "by the same (thing)."

24. Quam multos scriptores rerum suarum magnus ille Alexander
secum habuisse dicitur. Atque is tamen, cum in Sigeo ad Achillis tumulum
astitisset: "O fortunate," inquit "adulescens, qui tuae virtutis Homerum
praeconem inveneris!" Et vere: nam nisi Ilias illa exstitisset, idem
5   tumulus qui corpus eius contexerat nomen etiam obruisset. Quid?
Noster hic Magnus qui cum virtute fortunam adaequavit, nonne
Theophanem Mytilenaeum, scriptorem rerum suarum, in contione
militum civitate donavit, et nostri illi fortes viri, sed rustici ac milites,
dulcedine quadam gloriae commoti quasi participes eiusdem laudis
10   magno illud clamore approbaverunt?

SHORT ANSWER QUESTIONS

1. Comment on Cicero's word placement in describing Alexander in line 1.

   The two modifiers come before his name; the end word of the phrase creates a climax with the proper name.

2. When he stood at the tomb of Achilles, why did Alexander the Great call the hero "fortunate" (lines 3–4)? Why did Cicero agree with him (lines 4–5)?

   He had Homer to sing of his courage. If Homer had not made Troy famous in his epic, Achilles' name would have been buried along with his body.

3. Who was Theophanes (lines 7)? How did Pompey reward him and why were his soldiers so favorable to this reward (lines 7–10)?

   Theophanes was a writer from Mytilene in Greece who wrote about Pompey's achievements. Pompey granted him citizenship, and his soldiers felt that they felt that they, too, shared in the general's glory.

4. Find and give the Latin for a chiasmus in line 9.

   gloriae commoti quasi participes eiusdem laudis

Other Questions

1. Translate the first word of the section.

    "how"

2. Give the mood, usage, and translation for

    (a) *astitisset* (line 3)

        subjunctive, circumstantial clause, "had stood"

    (b) *inveneris* (line 4)

        subjunctive, relative clause of characteristic, "you (who) have found"

    (c) *exstitisset* (line 4)

        subjunctive, past contrary to fact conditional, "would have stood out"

    (d) *obruisset* (line 5)

        subjunctive, past contrary to fact conditional, "would have buried"

3. Give the case, the reason for that case, and reference for

    (a) *fortunate* (line 3)

        vocative, direct address, Achilles

    (b) *eius* (line 5)

        genitive, possession, Achilles

    (c) *suarum* (line 7)

        genitive, possession, Pompey

    (d) *illud* (line 10)

        accusative, direct object, the reward of citizenship given to Theophanes

25. Itaque, credo, si civis Romanus Archias legibus non esset, ut ab aliquo imperatore civitate donaretur perficere non potuit. Sulla cum Hispanos et Gallos donaret, credo, hunc petentem repudiasset. Quem nos in contione vidimus, cum ei libellum malus poeta de populo subiecisset, quod
5 epigramma in eum fecisset tantum modo alternis versibus longiusculis, statim ex eis rebus, quas tum vendebat, iubere ei praemium tribui—sed ea condicione ne quid postea scriberet. Qui sedulitatem mali poetae duxerit aliquo tamen praemio dignam, huius ingenium et virtutem in scribendo et copiam non expetisset?

SHORT ANSWER QUESTIONS

1. Is Cicero's use of *credo* (lines 1 and 3) genuine or sarcastic? Discuss briefly.

    Cicero uses *credo* sarcastically. The general Sulla rewarded a second-rate poet. Archias should have been able to enjoy the same treatment

2. Cicero cites an episode in which Sulla rewarded a bad poet.

    (a) What was the condition attached to the reward (lines 7)?

    The poet should stop writing.

    (b) Why might Sulla have sought out Archias instead (line 7–9)?

    Archias was a more accomplished poet.

    (c) *Alternis versibus longiusculis* (lines 5–6) refers to what poetic meter?

    elegiac couplet (alternate lines of hexameter and pentameter)

OTHER QUESTIONS

1. Give the mood and usage for

    (a) *esset* (line 1)

    subjunctive, present contrary to fact conditional

    (b) *repudiasset* (line 3)

    subjunctive, past contrary to fact conditional

2. To whom does each refer?

    (a) *hunc* (line 3)

    (Archias)

    (b) *ei* (line 4)

    Sulla

    (c) *Qui* (line 7)

    Sulla

    (d) *huius* (line 8)

    Archias

Essay Question

In sections 10 (below) and 25 (above), Cicero describes the granting of citizenship to recipients seemingly "less worthy" than Archias. Contrast these situations with that of Archias. Why does he seem "more worthy" of citizenship than the others? What tone is prevalent in both examples and why?

10. Quae cum ita sint, quid est quod de eius civitate dubitetis,
praesertim cum aliis quoque in civitatibus fuerit ascriptus? Etenim
cum mediocribus multis et aut nulla aut humili aliqua arte praeditis
gratuito civitatem in Graecia homines impertiebant, Reginos credo
5   aut Locrensis aut Neapolitanos aut Tarentinos, quod scaenicis
artificibus largiri solebant, id huic summa ingeni praedito gloria
noluisse! Quid? Cum ceteri non modo post civitatem datam sed
etiam post legem Papiam aliquo modo in eorum municipiorum tabulas
inrepserunt, hic qui ne utitur quidem illis in quibus est scriptus, quod
10   semper se Heracliensem esse voluit, reicietur?

Students should see the irony/sarcasm in the passage (*Quid? credo*, deliberative questions) and Cicero's desire to have the jurors feel guilty or remorseful for even considering a denial of citizenship to such a man. When mediocre men, actors, and a second-rate poet can become citizens, how can Romans exclude this very excellent poet who also followed the laws to attain citizenship?

26. Quid? a Q. Metello Pio, familiarissimo suo, qui civitate multos
donavit, neque per se neque per Lucullos impetravisset? qui praesertim
usque eo de suis rebus scribi cuperet ut etiam Cordubae natis poetis
pingue quiddam sonantibus atque peregrinum tamen auris suas dederet.

5   Neque enim est hoc dissimulandum quod obscurari non potest, sed prae
nobis ferendum: trahimur omnes studio laudis, et optimus quisque
maxime gloria ducitur. Ipsi illi philosophi etiam in eis libellis quos
de contemnenda gloria scribunt nomen suum inscribunt; in eo ipso
in quo praedicationem nobilitatemque despiciunt praedicari de se ac

10   nominari volunt.

Short Answer Questions

1. Why might Q. Metellus Pius have been of some help to Archias in obtaining citizenship (lines 1–2)?

   He was very close to him, and he had given it as a gift to many.

2. To what lengths had Marcellus gone to be glorified in verse (lines 2–4)?

   He even listened to poets born in Corduba (Hispania) who made thick, foreign sounds.

3. Translate lines 5–7 (*Neque . . . ducitur*) as literally as you can into good English.

   For this must not be hidden (a fact) which cannot be concealed but in front of us must be presented: we all are drawn by the desire for praise, and every very good person is led most greatly by glory.

4. Why might certain philosophers seem hypocritical about being glorified?

   They condemn being glorified while allowing, even wanting, their names to be made public (they want to be given credit publicly for their work).

OTHER QUESTIONS

1. Give the case, reason for that case, and a translation for *familiarissimo suo* (line 1).

   ablative, apposition to *Metello pio*, "his very close friend"

2. To whom does *se* (line 2) refer?

   Archias

3. What conjunction seems to be missing from the opening of the sentence? *qui praesertim* (line 2)?

   ***Cum* (since)**

4. Give the case and reason for that case for

   (a) *Cordubae* (line 3)

   locative, place where

   (b) *pingue* (line 4)

   accusative, modifies *quiddam*

   (c) *auris* (line 4)

   accusative, direct object

   (d) *se* (line 9). To what or whom does this pronoun refer?

   ablative with *de*, referring to the philosopher

27. Decimus quidem Brutus, summus vir et imperator, Acci, amicissimi sui, carminibus templorum ac monumentorum aditus exornavit suorum. Iam vero ille qui cum Aetolis Ennio comite bellavit Fulvius non dubitavit Martis manubias Musis consecrare.

5   Quare, in qua urbe imperatores prope armati poetarum nomen et Musarum delubra coluerunt, in ea non debent togati iudices a Musarum honore et a poetarum salute abhorrere.

SHORT ANSWER QUESTIONS

1. Why does Cicero bring the generals Decimus Brutus and Fulvius into his argument?

   Even as generals they honored the arts by decorating temples and monuments with poems and dedications to the Muses.

2. How does Cicero use their examples to provoke the jury? What figure of speech does he employ (line 4)? Give the Latin and English.

   Jury members (in togas) ought not to shun the Muses and poets. Martis: metonymy for war.

3. Who is *Ennio comite* (line 3) and in what context was he seen earlier?

   Ennius, the epic poet in section 22, who glorified Cato the Elder

OTHER QUESTIONS

1. Give the case and reason for that case for

   (a) *Acci* (line 1). Briefly identify this person.

      genitive, possession; author of tragedy, contemporary of Brutus

   (b) *aditus* (line 2)

      accusative, direct object

   (c) *Martis* (line 4)

      genitive, possession

   (d) *armati* (line 5), *togati* (line 6). What does each modify? How does Cicero highlight the contrast?

      nominative, modifies *imperatores* and *iudices* The contrast is highlighted by chiasmus (*imperatores . . . armati . . . togati iudices*).

ESSAY QUESTION

In sections 19 (below) and 27 (above), Cicero describes the treatment of the poet and literary artist. What universal examples and what specific persons are mentioned and why? Why do you think he included military generals in his argument? Be sure to cite the Latin (with English) that supports your ideas.

> **19.** Sit igitur, iudices, sanctum apud vos, humanissimos homines,
> hoc poetae nomen quod nulla umquam barbaria violavit. Saxa atque
> solitudines voci respondent, bestiae saepe immanes cantu flectuntur
> atque consistunt; nos instituti rebus optimis non poetarum voce moveamur?
> 5 Homerum Colophonii civem esse dicunt suum, Chii suum vindicant,
> Salaminii repetunt, Smyrnaei vero suum esse confirmant itaque etiam
> delubrum eius in oppido dedicaverunt, permulti alii praeterea pugnant
> inter se atque contendunt. Ergo illi alienum, quia poeta fuit, post mortem
> etiam expetunt; nos hunc vivum qui et voluntate et legibus noster est
> 10 repudiamus, praesertim cum omne olim studium atque omne ingenium
> contulerit Archias ad populi Romani gloriam laudemque celebrandam?
> Nam et Cimbricas res adulescens attigit et ipsi illi C. Mario qui durior
> ad haec studia videbatur iucundus fuit.

At the opening of 19, Cicero describes the effect of poetry on the natural world: animals, desolate places, even citing barbarians (to inflict more guilt/remorse? *Nos instituti rebus optimis . . .*). He contrasts the response of various Greek peoples who fought over identifying Homer as their own with the Romans' apparent apathy toward the poetic voice. Military victors (e.g., *Marius or Fulvius or Decimus Brutus) had an especially high status in the Roman world. To witness such generals (*durior,bellavit, prope armati*) embracing literature and poetry, *adorning temples and buildings with poetry, and cherishing the Muses, should be an incentive for toga-ed (synecdoche) jurymen to do the same. (Perhaps students will remember Cicero's famous phrase, *arma togae cedant,* "let arms yield to the toga.")

28. Atque ut id libentius faciatis, iam me vobis, iudices, indicabo
et de meo quodam amore gloriae nimis acri fortasse, verum tamen honesto
vobis confitebor. Nam quas res nos in consulatu nostro vobiscum simul
pro salute huius urbis atque imperi et pro vita civium proque universa re
5   publica gessimus, attigit hic versibus atque inchoavit. Quibus auditis,
quod mihi magna res et iucunda visa est, hunc ad perficiendum adornavi.
Nullam enim virtus aliam mercedem laborum periculorumque desiderat
praeter hanc laudis et gloriae. Qua quidem detracta, iudices, quid est
quod in hoc tam exiguo vitae curriculo et tam brevi tantis nos in laboribus
10   exerceamus?

Short Answer Questions

1. In the passage above, Cicero confesses to the jury one of his great desires. In a short essay, discuss how Cicero defends this desire and Archias' role in the pursuit of it.

    He confesses to a rather fierce love of glory, but it is an honorable one; he saved the city, state, and life of its citizens by revealing the Catilinarian Conspiracy; Archias has already begun to write verses about his deeds which Cicero heard, praised, and urged to completion.

2. To what specific event does *res nos in consulatu nostro* (line 3)?

    the Catilinarian Conspiracy.

3. What is meant by *magna res* (line 6)?

    Archias' writing about Cicero's role in the prosecution of Catiline

Other Questions

1. What part of speech is *libentius* (line 1)? Translate it.

    adverb, comparative; "more freely"

2. To whom or what does *hic* refer (line 5)?

    Archias

3. What construction is *Quibus auditis* (line 5)? What would be a good translation for it?

    ablative absolute; "When these things were heard"

4. Translate the sentence *Nullam . . . gloriae* (lines 7–8).

    "For virtue desires no other reward for its toils and dangers except this prize of praise and glory"

29. Certe, si nihil animus praesentiret in posterum, et si, quibus regionibus
vitae spatium circumscriptum est, isdem omnis cogitationes terminaret suas,
nec tantis se laboribus frangeret neque tot curis vigiliisque angeretur nec
totiens de ipsa vita dimicaret. Nunc insidet quaedam in optimo quoque
5   virtus, quae noctes ac dies animum gloriae stimulis concitat atque
admonet non cum vitae tempore esse dimittendam commemorationem
nominis nostri, sed cum omni posteritate adaequandam.

SHORT ANSWER QUESTIONS

1. According to Cicero, how is the mind responsible for its own feelings about hardship, anxiety, and the struggle for life itself (lines 1–4)?

   The mind is concerned about the future and does not limit itself to the boundaries of its own lifespan.

2. Describe the specific quality Cicero mentions in each noble person that accounts for such activity of the mind (lines 4–7).

   desire for glory

3. Cicero uses an abundance of time words in this passage to make his point about glory. Cite at least two or three words that refer to time and briefly discuss their impact on the section.

   ***posterum* (line 1), the future; *vitae spatium* (line 2), span of life; *noctes ac dies* (line 5), nights and days; *vitae tempore* (line 6), time of life; *posteritate* (line 7), the future. They emphasize the influence of time on how or if we are remembered. Time passes; do we along with it?**

OTHER QUESTIONS

1. Give the mood, usage, and translation for

   (a) *praesentiret* (line 1)

      subjunctive, present contrary to fact conditional; "should know beforehand"

   (b) *frangeret* (line 3)

      subjunctive, present contrary to fact conditional; "it would not break/crush"

2. What figure of speech is seen in lines 3–4 and how does it enhance the meaning of the passage?

   The anaphora (*nec . . . neque . . . nec*) emphasizes the number of concerns involved in securing glory for the future. The tricolon crescens has the same enhancing quality.

30. An vero tam parvi animi videamur esse omnes qui in re publica atque in his vitae periculis laboribusque versamur ut, cum usque ad extremum spatium nullum tranquillum atque otiosum spiritum duxerimus, nobiscum simul moritura omnia arbitremur? An statuas et imagines, non

5   animorum simulacra, sed corporum, studiose multi summi homines reliquerunt; consiliorum relinquere ac virtutum nostrarum effigiem nonne multo malle debemus summis ingeniis expressam et politam? Ego vero omnia quae gerebam iam tum in gerendo spargere me ac disseminare arbitrabar in orbis terrae memoriam sempiternam. Haec vero sive a meo

10   sensu post mortem afutura est, sive, ut sapientissimi homines putaverunt, ad aliquam animi mei partem pertinebit, nunc quidem certe cogitatione quadam speque delector.

Short Answer Questions

1. In this chapter, Cicero poses questions and makes a personal comment about the afterlife. How and why does he wish to alter the custom of *imagines* (lines 4–7)? What hope sustains and delights him as he considers life after death (lines 9–12)?

   We should be concerned with leaving images (memories) of our ideals and mental qualities/intellect for posterity, not just of our physical qualities. Whether he has an awareness of this memory of his deeds or not after death, he is sustained by the thought and the hope that there is the possibility.

Other Questions

1. Give the mood, usage, and translation for

   (a) *videamur* (line 1)

   subjunctive, deliberative question, "do we seem"

   (b) *duxerimus* (line 3)

   subjunctive, circumstantial clause, "we have brought'

   (c) *arbitremur* (line 4)

   subjunctive, result, "we think"

2. Give the case and reason for that case for

   (a) *animi* (line 1)

   genitive, description

   (b) *quae* (line 8)

   accusative, direct object

   (c) *haec* (line 9). To what does it refer?

   nominative, subject; *memoria*

3. What part of speech is *multo* and what is its case and reason for that case (line 7)?

   adjective, ablative, degree of difference with *malle* (with comparative force), "prefer by much (=much prefer)"

Essay Question

In sections 14 (below) and 30 (above), Cicero uses the word *imagines* to strengthen his discussion on the value of literature. Identify how he uses the term in each section: what function did they serve and under what conditions? How did Cicero himself make use of them in his own life? Does he seem consistent in each discussion? Use specific Latin from each section to support your statements.

> **14.** Nam nisi multorum praeceptis multisque litteris mihi ab
> adulescentia suasissem nihil esse in vita magno opere expetendum nisi
> laudem atque honestatem, in ea autem persequenda omnis cruciatus corporis,
> omnia pericula mortis atque exsili parvi esse ducenda, numquam me pro
> 5   salute vestra in tot ac tantas dimicationes atque in hos profligatorum
> hominum cotidianos impetus obiecissem. Sed pleni omnes sunt libri, plenae
> sapientium voces, plena exemplorum vetustas; quae iacerent in tenebris
> omnia, nisi litterarum lumen accederet. Quam multas nobis imagines non
> solum ad intuendum verum etiam ad imitandum fortissimorum virorum
> 10   expressas scriptores et Graeci et Latini reliquerunt! Quas ego mihi
> semper in administranda re publica proponens animum et mentem meam
> ipsa cogitatione hominum excellentium conformabam.

Students should draw a distinction between 14.6–7 ("portraits, examples") from the writers and 30.4–5 ("statues, funeral masks") referring to the physical representations made of individuals. Both are to be used (as did Cicero) in times of struggles, service to the state, even when risking one's life for excellence. The first exalts writers for giving the public examples not only to look at (read about) but also to emulate; the second encourages his audience to go beyond mere physical commemoratives of the self after death to include "images" of qualities of character and of the mind. Cicero does give himself credit in each instance for (a) following the examples afforded by writers and (b) hoping to keep a memory of his accomplishments in the minds of the public by the very doing of his deeds. (In the latter example, he confesses that he does not know if he will have a perception after death of how he is remembered but he at least has hope.)

31 Quare conservate, iudices, hominem pudore eo quem amicorum
videtis comprobari cum dignitate, tum etiam vetustate, ingenio autem tanto
quantum id convenit existimari, quod summorum hominum iudiciis
expetitum esse videatis, causa vero eius modi quae beneficio legis,
5   auctoritate municipi, testimonio Luculli, tabulis Metelli comprobetur.
Quae cum ita sint, petimus a vobis, iudices, si qua non modo humana
verum etiam divina in tantis ingeniis commendatio debet esse, ut eum
qui vos, qui vestros imperatores, qui populi Romani res gestas semper
ornavit, qui etiam his recentibus nostris vestrisque domesticis periculis
10   aeternum se testimonium laudis daturum esse profitetur, quique est ex
eo numero qui semper apud omnis sancti sunt habiti itaque dicti, sic in
vestram accipiatis fidem ut humanitate vestra levatus potius quam
acerbitate violatus esse videatur.

SHORT ANSWER QUESTIONS

1. What is the significance of the word *Quare* (line 1)? For what is the audience being prepared? What is this section of a speech called and what is its purpose?

    The word *Quare* (line 1) begins the conclusion of the speech. The audience is cued for the *peroratio*, wherein the speaker delivers a summation, in this case with a final appeal for Archias' citizenship.

2. What do the friends of Archias contribute to his honor (lines 1–3)?

    They contribute their status and many long years of friendship.

3. To what does *municipi* (line 5) refer, both generally and specifically?

    Small communities with restricted citizenship within the Roman domain (here, Heraclea).

4. What proof does Cicero repeat in his summary argument to prove his case (lines 3–5)?

    Cicero repeats the testimony of representatives from Heraclea, the law, the testimony of Lucullus, and the archives of Metellus.

5. Where is the focus of the section placed by the repetition of *qui* five times in lines 7–10?

    The focus is on Archias who has done all these things for Roman glory.

6. Give Cicero's rationale why the jury should offer Archias its trust (lines 7–13).

    He has celebrated Roman generals and deeds of the Roman people, and promises more in the future.

Other Questions

1. Give the case and reason for that case for

   (a) *pudore* (line 1)

      ablative, description

   (b) *quae* (line 4)

      nominative, subject

   (c) *qua* (line 6)

      nominative, modifies *commendatio*

   (d) *omnis* (line 11)

      accusative with *apud*

2. Translate *sic . . . videatur* (lines 11–13).

   "that you accept him in such a way that he would seem raised by your humanity rather than violated by your bitterness"

32. Quae de causa pro mea consuetudine breviter simpliciterque
dixi, iudices, ea confido probata esse omnibus; quae a foro aliena
iudicialique consuetudine et de hominis ingenio et communiter
de ipso studio locutus sum, ea, iudices, a vobis spero esse in bonam
5   partem accepta, ab eo qui iudicium exercet, certo scio.

SHORT ANSWER QUESTIONS

1. Translate this section as literally as you can into good English.

   "Therefore, I have spoken briefly in accordance with my customary manner, jurors, those things I trust are commended to all: those things which, foreign from the forum and judicial custom, I have spoken both about the man's talent together with (his) pursuit of learning itself. Those things, jurors, I hope have been welcomed by you in good part; I know for certain by him who oversees the trial."

2. To whom does *qui iudicium exercet* (line 5) refer? What relation is he to Cicero?

   It refers to the praetor in charge of the case. The praetor is Cicero's brother, Quintus Cicero.

OTHER QUESTIONS

1. Give the case and reason for that case for

   (a) *Quae* (line 1)

      accusative, direct object

   (b) *aliena* (line 2)

      accusative, modifies *quae* (direct object of *locutus sum*)

   (c) *iudicalique* (line 3)

      ablative, modifies *consuetudine*

   (d) *ea* (line 4)

      accusative, subject of indirect statement

   (e) *vobis* (line 4)

      ablative, agent

   (f) *iudicium* (line 5)

      accusative, direct object

2. What part of speech are *breviter, simpliciter,* and *communiter* (lines 1–3)?

   adverbs

SELECTED BIBLIOGRAPHY

I list here only the sources that have been of use to me in the writing of this book. This bibliography is by no means a complete list of all the books and sources I have consulted but includes those I thought were most relevant for teachers of the *pro Archia*. Especially helpful are Anthony Everitt's biography of Cicero and Hall and Bond's video of speech performances. Both provide an immediate entry into the political and personal world of Cicero.

Everitt, Anthony. *Cicero: The Life and Times of Rome's Greatest Politician*. New York: Random House, 2003.

Gotoff, Harold C. *Cicero's Elegant Style: An Analysis of the Pro Archia*. Urbana, Illinois: The University of Illinois Press, 1979.

Hall, Jon, and Robin Bond. *Performing Cicero's Speeches: An Experimental Workshop*. Wauconda, Illinois: Bolchazy-Carducci Publishers, Inc., 2002. (VHS)

Kennedy, George. *The Art of Rhetoric in the Roman World*. Princeton: Princeton University Press, 1972.

Kunzer, Paul E. *Vocabulary of Cicero's Archias*. Brookline Village: Branden Press, 1983.

Mitchel, T.N. *Cicero: The Ascending Years*. New Haven: Yale University Press, 1979.

————. *Cicero: The Senior Statesman*. New Haven: Yale University Press, 1991.

Sherwin White, A.N. *The Roman Citizenship*. 2nd ed. Oxford: The Clarendon Press, 1973.

Sihler, E.G. *Cicero of Arpinum*. New Haven: Yale University Press, 1914.

West, Grace Starry. *Cicero, Pro Archia*. 2nd ed. Bryn Mawr: Bryn Mawr College Press, 1995.

CICERO:
PRO ARCHIA POETA ORATIO
2nd Edition
Student Text by Steven M. Cerutti

Cicero's Pro Archia Poeta Oratio is one of the best defenses of literature and the humanities. Cerutti's edition provides a comprehensive treatment of grammatical issues with a keen analysis of the rhetorical devices Cicero wove into the fabric of the oration.

This edition combines

- the Latin text
- running vocabulary and commentary
- a brief bibliography
- glossary of proper names and places
- glossary of terms
- general vocabulary

An excellent edition for the AP* and college classroom

Student Text: xxviii + 132 pp (2006) Paperback 6" x 9" ISBN 978-0-86516-642-4

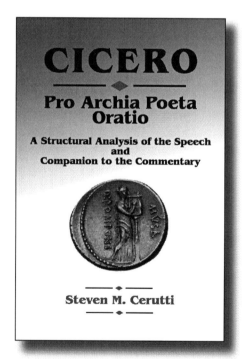

CICERO:
PRO ARCHIA POETA ORATIO
A Structural Analysis of the Speech and Companion to the Commentary
Steven Cerutti

The "COMPANION" was written to accompany *Cicero: Pro Archia Poeta Oratio*, but makes an excellent independent resource for all *Pro Archia* texts.

Comprehensive diagrams and detailed sentence-by-sentence analysis provide the student with a reliable road map through the periodic structure of the Ciceronian sentence.

Features:

- Introduction, "Reading the Diagrams"
- Latin text with same-page and facing
  - Translation
  - Notes & Discussion
  - Latin text in sentence diagrams

xii + 118 pp (1999) Paperback 6" x 9" ISBN 978-0-86516-439-0

BOLCHAZY-CARDUCCI PUBLISHERS, INC.
WWW.BOLCHAZY.COM

CICERO ANCILLARY MATERIALS

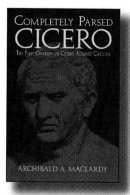

COMPLETELY PARSED CICERO: The First Oration of Cicero Against Catiline
Archibald A. Maclardy

Completely Parsed Cicero is an irreplaceable, primary resource for educators. The complete text of *In Catilinam* I, an interlinear translation, and an accompanying, more polished translation are just part of this goldmine. At the bottom of each page below the text, each Latin word is completely parsed. The commentary includes useful references to the revised grammars of Bennett, Gildersleeve, Allen and Greenough, and Harkness and delves into word derivations and word frequencies, making this volume helpful for the competent reader of Latin as well as the novice.

A new introduction by Steven M. Cerutti of East Carolina University provides guidelines for the use of this resource by high school Latin teachers and educators at all levels.

Features: • Complete Latin text of *In Catilinam* I • Complete interlinear translation of the Latin text • A more elegant translation in the margin next to the text • A full grammatical, syntactical, and etymological commentary on each word in the text • An introduction that provides an exposition of the historical circumstances surrounding the Catilinarian conspiracy of 63 BCE

272 pp. (1902, reprint 2004) Paperback, ISBN 978-0-86516-590-8

CICERO THE PATRIOT
Rose Williams

Light-hearted in tone but faithful to the facts, this volume interweaves Cicero's private life and feelings with the development of his public life and literary output. Supplementary materials make this an invaluable resource for both students and teachers.

Features: • Complete description of events and historical circumstances of Cicero's life • Timeline of events and publication of Cicero's works • Glossary of terms • One-page summary of Cicero's life

Teacher's Manual Features: • Suggestions for study enrichment • Sample report topics • Further information for the teacher • Thought questions for students • Quick questions to test comprehension

Student Text: vi + 92 pp. (2004) Paperback 6" x 9" ISBN 978-0-86516-587-8
Teacher's Manual: xi + 74 pp. (2004) Paperback 6" x 9" ISBN 978-0-86516-588-5

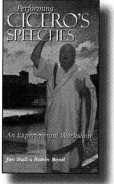

PERFORMING CICERO'S SPEECHES: An Experimental Workshop
a video by Jon Hall and Robin Bond

How exactly did Cicero perform his speeches? This video uses guidelines on voice and gesture from rhetorical treatises to reconstruct Cicero's oratorical delivery in a theatrical workshop environment.

Features: • Passages discussed and performed from six of Cicero's speeches: *Pro Caelio*, Pro *Milone*, Pro *Ligario*, Pro *Archia*, *In Catilinam* 2, *Philippics* 6 • Booklet with complete Latin texts and translations • Bibliography • Restored Classical Pronunciation! But much more!

VHS Videotape (32 minutes) and Booklet (2003) ISBN 978-0-86516-488-8

THE LOCK
Benita Kane Jaro

The Lock, though it is a completely independent novel, continues the portrait of the collapsing Roman society of the late Republic so brilliantly depicted in *The Key*. The principal figures of the age—poets, scholars, soldiers, politicians, powerful political women, even slaves, Julius Caesar, Cicero, Pompey the Great—all make their appearance and play out their fateful struggle.

> Benita Kane Jaro is an exciting writer of great skill and grace. Courage, too...The result is a powerful and moving story, as freshly minted as today's news and as haunting as the deepest memory.
>
> –George Garrett

> If there is to be a worthy successor to Mary Renault, or to Marguerite Yourcenar, it may be Benita Kane Jaro.
>
> –Doris Grumbach

xxii + 282 pp, original illustrations (2002) Paperback ISBN 978-0-86516-535-9

BOLCHAZY-CARDUCCI PUBLISHERS, INC.
WWW.BOLCHAZY.COM

OTHER CICERO TEXTS

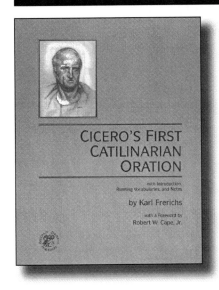

CICERO'S FIRST CATILINARIAN ORATION
Karl Frerichs

Cicero's First Catilinarian speech is now available in a practical and inexpensive annotated edition for third-year Latin students. In light of existing textbooks, Karl Frerichs' edition has several important and distinguishing strengths:

- Clear, tripartite page layout for text, vocabulary and notes on facing pages
- Running vocabulary separate from notes and complete vocabulary at the end
- Introduction and Glossary of Terms and Figures of Speech provide basic biographical, historical, and rhetorical background
- Maps and illustrations

> Even where his notes were not quite all that some of the students needed, Frerichs enabled them to ask intelligent questions about their problems. His historical comments, while necessarily brief, provided us with convenient points of departure for fuller class discussions.
> —Dale Grote, *The Classical Outlook*

80 pp. (1997, Reprint 2000) Paperback, ISBN 978-0-86516-341-6

ON OLD AGE: DE SENECTUTE
Marcus Tullius Cicero
Latin text with notes and vocabulary
Charles E. Bennett

On Old Age was the first ancient text in translation that publisher Benjamin Franklin chose for release in America. He was rightfully proud of his now much admired 1743 edition and anticipated, with his customary wry wit, that reading it would give pleasure:

> I have, Gentle Reader, as thou seest, printed this Piece of Cicero's in a large and fair Character, that those who begin to think on the Subject of OLD AGE, (which seldom happens till their Sight is somewhat impair'd by its Approaches) may not, in Reading, by the Pain small Letters give the Eyes, feel the Pleasure of the Mind in the least allayed.

Franklin was not alone among American patriots in his praise of Cicero, about whom John Adams remarked: "All ages of the world have not produced a greater statesman and philosopher combined."

Cicero's On Old Age speaks as directly to all of us today—those approaching old age as well as the younger—as it did to Franklin and Adams. Long considered one of Cicero's most engaging, charming, and readable treatises, it quite simply transcends time. Cicero steps out of the persona of the "great man" and examines, with superlative clarity, the challenges all human beings must one day face.

This edition features

- Latin text
- Notes (at back, referenced to page and line numbers)
- Vocabulary
- Index of Proper Names

viii + 226 pp (1922 Allyn and Bacon; Reprinted with Permission 1985, 1990, 2002)
6" x 9" Paperback ISBN 978-0-86516-001-9

BOLCHAZY-CARDUCCI PUBLISHERS, INC.
www.BOLCHAZY.com

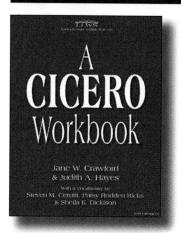
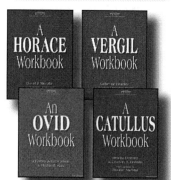